SIMPLY SPIRIT

A Personal Insight
By Gloria Pyne

Copyright © 2020 by Gloria Pyne
Cover Design by John Hathway
All Rights Reserved.

ISBN 9798568347385

Acknowledgement and sincere thanks
to Michelle Milner-Eradhun for
typography & publishing support.

To Kathleen,

I hope you enjoy the book
Shine Bright

Love
Gloria
xx

Contents

Introduction	1
Chapter 1	3
Chapter 2	16
Chapter 3	33
Chapter 4	41
Chapter 5	49
Chapter 6	57
Chapter 7	70
Chapter 8	81
Chapter 9	92
Chapter 10	102
Chapter 11	113
Chapter 12	128
Chapter 13	136
Chapter 14	146
Chapter 15	160

Introduction

In this world we live in today there are many changes happening, I believe one of the most important of all is our change in our spirituality, a necessary change to change the world we live in and become the spiritual beings we were created to be on this earth.

With this book I hope to bring a greater knowledge of spirituality, not as a religion but as a way of life, to bring an understanding, much needed today, and the knowledge to deal with what is happening to us all in this ever-changing world.

The realms of the spirit world are coming closer to us, we are all reaching a higher spirituality and even though there is so much chaos, pain and suffering and evil on this planet, we shall and must rise to a higher plane of existence to enable the world to become a better and safer place to live.

So, it is time to awaken us all and connect ourselves to not only our own spirit but to the world of spirit.

I write this book to help in understanding all things spiritual and to enlighten us all to the beauty and love of spirit.

I hope that through this book I can clarify some of the most import issues, how we can work with the spirit world, understand how to communicate but most of all take away our fears.

I dedicate this book to my family and friends, but most of all to Spirit who have inspired me, taught me, guided me and given me their unconditional love.

Chapter 1

I don't know about you, but I have found that there is so much confusion regarding spirit, so much misconception about the role and the part that spirit play in our lives. There is also so much fear a fear of the 'unknown' which has, over generations, been brought about by too many horror films and misguided ideas and indeed horror stories to ignite the imagination.

Now I'm not saying that there is not an element of evil around us, absolutely not. For in this world and the next there is both good and evil, for where there is good there is bad, where there is love there is hate, such is the nature of life in all forms.

However, the pathway of spirituality is a simple one, albeit not always an easy one, for human nature is what it is and none of us are perfect; we have a long, long way to go before that will happen I'm afraid! Neither are we expected to be perfect, we are here to do the best we can to listen to the good voice inside of us and to do our best to act upon it, however hard that may be at times!

So, let me begin with a simple version of why we are here on this earth…

We all come from the spirit world. It is our natural home, it is where we came from and will inevitably go back to. As to which level we return to is of our own making to a degree, for firstly we have lessons to learn from being on the earth.

We are here to evolve, and some are here to make a difference. All that is asked of us from spirit is to do our very best to be good and decent human beings. We are watched over by spirit and each of us has a 'Spiritual Helper' to guide us and help us; truth is that so many do not or indeed do not know how to hear them, but they are truly inspirational if we open our minds and our hearts to them.

We do of course have free will, which is much respected by spirit, but they are always on hand to give a helping hand when we need it, be it for making choices on our pathway or generally guiding us to do what is right. Doing what is right is actually the most natural thing for we humans, we have a conscience and although most of us listen to that inner voice, there are many who will ignore it much to the cost of others and to themselves.

So many of us are always asking for help from spirit, how many times have you raised your eyes upwards and asked to be shown what to do in all matters concerning your life? We of course hope that some miracle will happen and we will hear that voice tell us exactly what to do, but in truth most people cannot 'hear' or have not learnt how to hear. But spirit can and do give us their help by way of inspiration.

Quite often after seeking help from them, some time later we suddenly have that 'light bulb' moment when ideas seem to just pop into our heads, then there are cries of *"Why didn't I think of that before*". Many a time it is spirit just waiting to find that moment when they can get through to us and make us listen and indeed answer our pleas for help and guidance. Such is the wonder of spirit and of course we take credit ourselves, oblivious to those that are helping us.

Many people ask why some can communicate with spirit whilst others cannot. Well, firstly I have to say that each and every one of us has the ability to do so in one way or another. We are of course connected as we are indeed spirit ourselves, sadly when we are born to this earth we seem to forget how to as we get older; the reason I say when we get older is that truthfully all children can see, hear and feel spirit.

How many of you that have young children hear them talking to what adults refer to as their 'imaginary friend', when in fact 9 times out of 10 they certainly aren't imaginary but real spirit visitors. It could be a family member or other spirit children that come to play and keep them company, it is the most natural thing in the world for children to talk to them. Sadly, children have a habit of shutting off as they grow older. Sometimes it's because adults feel uncomfortable with the notion that the child is talking to people that are no longer here and that they can neither see nor hear them causes a feeling of unease. Many dismiss the idea totally and convince children that it is all in their imagination or a subject that is taboo and not to be spoken of. Wouldn't it be wonderful if we could accept that they can? If we all did, all children would grow with a greater knowledge of the spirit world and a greater spiritual understanding. It would be accepted as the most natural thing in the world, which it truly is, but most importantly children would become stronger and kinder, then the world would be a better place to live in and indeed none of us would fear the 'unknown', for it would no longer be unknown! Food for thought...

I have been asked many times how I have come to learn and understand the world of spirit. Well, I have to admit it has been a long process and not one without much dedication and perseverance both from myself and from spirit! But it's a very worthwhile journey, and not one without some degree of frustration I might add, but a journey well worth taking and embarking on. It has changed my life for the better in so many different ways, as it does for many who walk this path if indeed it is done with the right intentions and the right motivation.

I have found my spiritual journey a pure delight, to be able to open doorways to another dimension and to gain insight into the truth and where we come from has been a real eye opener for me, and a pleasure. To be able to communicate with those in the spirit world, not just the Guides and amazing teachers that are there to work with us and indeed share their great wisdom and knowledge, but to be able to talk to my own family that have passed is truly a great comfort to me.

When you lose someone close to you it is hard

to come to terms with that loss for us all, so to be able to converse with them still and know that they are with us is truly a comfort.

I started working for spirit over 30 years ago and I cannot lie, it hasn't always been an easy process to develop the abilities we all have. But I believe in some, the ability and desire to develop is stronger and when it is strong within you, it becomes a necessity as it did for me and has now become my passion. I had many experiences when I first began my pathway and that led me to begin my own process of development, some of which I will share with you a little later on.

I have now successfully developed all three senses to enable me to communicate with those in spirit; I can see, hear and sense spirit with me and around me. When I say 'see' and 'hear', it is not necessarily in the conventional sense. I see some energies with my eyes, I can see light and outlines of spirit and once I connect I get a vision in my head of what a person looked like or even images of places, houses, buildings or areas. It's a bit like having a television screen in your head which shows me pictures I need to see to be able to pass on the information to people. It is the same with hearing, I hear voices in my head not in my ear, although it has happened on rare occasions when I haven't been listening and spirit have wanted to attract my attention! The wonderful thing about having all these abilities is that it is easier to get the information that spirit wish to impart when it is given to you in different ways, and also that visual transfer of information and indeed verbal communication brings greater clarity.

What so many people these days need to understand is that our connection and communication with those that have passed and reside in the spirit world is the most natural thing. We are indeed spirit ourselves and therefore it is normal to be aware of spirit and to connect with those that love us. We should never be afraid of our family and friends that have passed to the world of spirit, they love us unconditionally and have no desire to harm us; they loved us when they were here on earth and will continue that love in spirit - much enhanced I might add.

When we talk to them (as we all do, don't we?), we ask for help from them, wishing they were still here with us, we ask for guidance in our daily lives and in making decisions, but get frustrated when we don't 'hear' a response. We simply need to learn how to listen.

Now I know that may sound easier than it is and of course that is true as many of us have never learnt how to open the lines of communication. But there is a simple way. When a question is asked of spirit for guidance, wait a while, ask no more questions and carry on as normal with your day. It is the searching for the answer that often blocks the ability to listen and hear; when you are relaxed and probably least expecting it you will be given your answer by way of inspiration, a thought planted by them into your mind, very cleverly too I might add, and usually we take credit then for solving our own problems! But rest assured when you ask them for help in any way, they will do all they can to give us the help and guidance we need.

The true pathway to connection with spirit is actually a very simple one, spirit will teach us in the easiest and simplest ways. Too often it is us that complicate matters by wishing to run before we can walk, and many people turn to the internet and books to find the truth but unfortunately, it isn't always out there or indeed the truth! Many sites claim to know all about the workings of spirit but in fact have never communicated directly with them so how can they know the truth? Hearsay and other peoples' writings? I have found that many such sites make it all the more confusing.

Spirit only wish us to learn the truth, and in my experience, have taught me much about the spirit world and spirit directly and simply. Do we really need to know at this stage whether we are Starseeds, Pleiadians, Orions from another planet or universe? As interesting as it may sound, I truly believe we need to start at the beginning, learn the simplicity of how and why we communicate, who and what we are and how we can make a difference to the planet we are living on, because we can make a difference. It's about listening to the inner you, your own spirit that is your conscience which is always trying to tell us the right thing to do, but sadly many do not listen even to themselves.

We talk much about intuition and our 'gut feelings', again this is our inner self, our spirit trying to show us the way forward, but how often do we listen to it? No, we shrug it off and ignore it only to find ourselves going along the wrong pathway with the wrong people in our lives and doing the wrong things. If only we listened to ourselves, we would make better choices for us and for those in our lives and indeed in the world, for we truly need to change the way the world is today.

If you ask spirit to show you and guide you, they will of course, they can connect with you and touch you in ways we do not always understand. Just as they are spirit, we are too, and the connection is always there. The other thing to remember is that we have free will and spirit will never interfere with that, if we need their help it is gladly given, but we have to ask to allow them to help us and show us the way forward in our lives.

We need to understand and remember that spirit feel nothing but love for us and show us nothing but love too. The difference being is that they show us unconditional love, they expect nothing in return which is not always the way with the human race sadly. But I do believe and will always believe that there is more good on this earth than bad, more love than hate, and that is what will sustain us and eventually allow us to move forward.

However, where there is goodness and love there is always the alternative and that is so not just on this earth but in the spiritual realms too - another dimension that is out there that harbours evil and hatred, I will cover that a little later.

Chapter 2

I think it's probably an idea to give you a little information about me. Like many, I saw things, and saw spirit as a child, as do all children. I must admit though, it wasn't a constant occurrence and to be honest most experiences I do not remember fully; I mean, how many of us truly remember childhood experiences, especially from when we were very young? Memories often come from what we are told to us by our parents, and yes I remember certain events, usually those that were more profound of course. However, I do remember stages of my life and certain encounters that were indeed memorable.

When I was around 9 or 10 years old I had an amazing encounter with a spirit at my local community hall. I was there in the local choir practising when I needed to go to the ladies; the toilets were upstairs, and it was a very narrow winding staircase I had to ascend. As I reached the stairs, I saw a lovely and very elegant lady coming down the stairwell, so I waited for her to come down and watched her as she smiled at me.

I remember feeling very calm as I watched her gracefully glide down the staircase, I thought she was wearing very odd clothing, a long skirt, a high-necked ruffled collar blouse, very Victorian I remember thinking. It took a minute or two to then realise that she wasn't walking down the stairs but floating! I stepped back and then saw her disappear before my eyes. Well, I have to admit I was rather scared and ran back to my class as white as a sheet and shaking!

This was my first memorable encounter with the previous owner of the house we were in, her name is Mary and to this day she still visits the house, which ironically is where I now run a spiritual Centre with my colleagues and have got to know her very well and am used to her frequent visits.

It was again when I was 16 years old that I found

spirit seemed to be attracted to me, they also enjoyed showing themselves to me and those I was with at the time. From the age of 17 I went travelling, and although I had a number of spiritual encounters along the way, I was able to 'shut them out' for most of the time.

When I reached my mid to latter 20's, well then things really began to hot up! From this stage on I had frequent experiences and I must admit not all were pleasant either. At the time I lived in North Wales in a guest house on the top floor, and one day my neighbour decided to use a Ouija Board of the homemade variety. I was very against this as they had consumed copious amounts of alcohol at the time, which is definitely not a good idea to be summoning spirits whilst under the influence!

However, I was outvoted and felt very uncomfortable at the thought of it, but they pressed on anyway. To begin with, I refused to participate and agreed to watch. As they tried and tried, nothing much was happening with the glass on the table. I was goaded to join in and eventually relented. Strangely enough when I placed my finger on the glass, off it went spelling out all manner of messages and answers to questions from those at the table, much to the delight of everyone. Until it seems our spirit visitor became tired of this and decided not to play anymore, much to my relief I hasten to add.

The problem with this was that for a number of weeks after the event we had some very disturbing nights. It started with noises of someone stomping up and down the stairs when the house was basically empty, with the exception of three rooms on the top floor - very unnerving and also frustrating when trying to sleep. Then lights would go on and off, the worst was the knocking on doors, especially mine! I did get very annoyed at times and eventually shouted at our intruder to stop; much to my surprise it did. Our spirit visitor was also prone to move things in the flats, for example my neighbour would come home to find the whole room ransacked with no signs of anyone having broken in. It was time to confront our rampant spirit and get it to leave.

For the last time we decided to re-visit the board to find out who was causing all the commotion. It turned out it was a young man who had taken his own life many, many, years before by drowning himself. It also transpired that he had taken a liking to me and wanted to spend time with me, and when I reminded him that he was no longer of this world, he replied that he wanted me to join him in his world and also suggested I do so in the same manner that he had passed! Well, that was enough for me. I instantly cleared the board, destroyed the glass and letters and vowed never to use the Ouija board again. Thankfully, the house went quiet afterwards, and remained that way.

I had a number of encounters after that experience and realised that spirit were trying to tell me something. I moved a few times and each time I did it brought different types of encounters with spirit, but mostly they became more visual. I was woken up on a number of occasions by someone touching me or shaking me which in itself was not only very frustrating but also pretty scary at the time.

However, I did have a more pleasant visit. I was woken up in the middle of the night by the sound of footsteps in my bedroom - having had a number of these experiences I was afraid to turn round. The bedclothes began to lift off my shoulders and I felt a hand on the back of my neck. I have to say I suddenly felt an overwhelming calming feeling. The hand moved away and my bedclothes replaced, as if to tuck me in, I heard footsteps again and felt brave enough to look round, of course there was no one there - but I realised then that my visitors were looking after me and all my fears left me.

It was shortly after that that I returned to my family home in Hertfordshire, and that is when I realised that I needed to embrace the gifts that I and indeed we all have, and learn how to use them properly. I joined a development circle, and it took roughly two years to learn to be able to accept and enhance my abilities to a level where I could use them properly. I was fortunate enough to learn quickly and it became a true passion for me, I loved being able to talk to people in the spirit world to be able to see them, hear their voices and feel them around me, it was amazing.

As I progressed I moved into different areas of spiritual work, but I was more than happy to work alongside them and progress to whatever work they chose for me to do, and oh my, I certainly wasn't prepared at that time for what was to come. Since the start of my journey I have moved into areas I never dreamed of, and shortly afterwards I left and I started teaching others to control and develop their abilities and run my own circle. But before I left my first circle, I had another eye-opening experience.

On my last evening I went to tell my circle

leader that I was leaving. The reason I was leaving was partly because he had brought his new girlfriend into the circle, which was no problem in itself I might add, but she was a very controlling and jealous person; when I say jealous it was mostly of other people's abilities and she seemed to have taken a dislike to me. It had also caused a number of people to feel uncomfortable in the group and one of the keys to a successful circle is that everyone feels comfortable with each other as it becomes a very close and personal thing.

Also I, amongst others were being held back and I was no longer allowed to do the work I had been doing, and so after a few months of this I decided it was time for me to move on. My spirit Guides had also told me it was time, so it was time to go.

I remember very clearly the events of that night. I was nervous having to tell my teacher that it was time to move on and truly hoped he would not ask me the reasons why. My Guides reassured me that they were with me and all would be well, and when I arrived everyone else was in our usual room together but he was upstairs. After being invited up to see him, I went up the stairs. I got to the top of the stairs and something made me stop there, I could see him in the doorway of the room, so I blurted out that I was leaving. He was quite upset to hear my news and asked the question I had been dreading… "Why?". So I told him the truth. I explained that I didn't feel that his girlfriend and I were getting on too well and I also didn't want the others in the group to feel the tensions growing, and I felt it was time for me to move on. He spent a few minutes trying to convince me to stay, and as he spoke, I heard a noise from the end of the hallway. It turned out his girlfriend had come into the hallway and had been listening to our conversation - and had clearly got very angry! The next thing I knew, she was charging down the hallway shouting obscenities at me. For a moment I thought oh my God she's going to attack me! All of a sudden it was almost as if everything went into slow motion. I heard my Guides voice say to me *"Don't move!"*. I could see her face contorted with anger, but I did as I was told, and as she came at me, I saw a bright light appear in front of me as if a wall had been placed between us, and as she hit the wall she was knocked back. Well, the look of shock on her face was, as you can imagine quite profound, she had just hit an invisible wall!

I can tell you now I too was shocked, but of course extremely impressed with spirit for protecting me. There she stayed, on the other side of the wall, staring at me as I calmly walked away. I said my goodbyes to the group and explained it was time for me to move on, but I wished them all well. What surprised me was that as I got to the door there were three other people behind me, and they told me that they were coming with me. I wasn't sure what I was going to do let alone what they were going to do, and that's when spirit told me I needed to start my own circle and teach. From that day on I haven't stopped teaching or indeed ever underestimated the power of spirit.

On the subject of spirit Guides, I am often asked *"Who is my spirit Guide?"*. Well to be totally honest not everyone has one, many people are told that they have a spirit guide but in truth Guides are teachers. I asked spirit a long time ago if everyone has a spirit Guide and I was told no, but we do all have spiritual Helpers - many would call them Guardian Angels. It is more logical, as spirit explained to me, that if a person has no desire to develop and enhance their psychic abilities, why would they need a Guide? Why would they need these wonderful teachers to help them connect and grow spiritually if they have no desire to do so? If we decide we wish to do so, then a Guide is assigned to teach us. Regardless of this, we do all have Helpers with us from the spirit world to show us the way forward and to inspire us to be better people and indeed be kinder to each other.

On the subject of spirit Guides, should you decide to progress spiritually and indeed decide you wish to work for spirit, it is important to learn to develop your abilities in a safe and protected way. To develop oneself is actually quite difficult and can cause a lot of distress if it becomes out of control. In my experience as a teacher, I have helped a number of people who have found themselves in this situation. This is through no fault of their own, but through either misguided practices, usually sourced from information found on the internet and books, or through others that have never learnt the true way of spirit themselves.

The greatest teachers for your development are indeed spirit themselves, but of course one has to learn to connect properly to be able to communicate to further learn from them. So, the best way is to start in a development circle which is run by a Medium, preferably one who has been working for some time and has a greater understanding of the spirit world, and also someone that can give you the protection, insight and guidance you need whilst you learn to grow.

Textbook Mediumship doesn't always work; the greatest and strongest way to develop your abilities will come from spirit, the knowledge should be directly from them through your teacher and ultimately to you directly. There are no better teachers than spirit themselves of course, for they have the truth and first-hand experience. I have tried over the years to read books on spirituality, Mediumship and the like, but I often found them confusing. Initially when I first started my development, I thought I needed to rush out and buy myself some books on the subject, as I didn't know or understand a lot at that time. I was firmly told by my Guides not to and that I didn't need them as many are indeed confusing, contradictory and misleading - and most of all unnecessary as everything that I needed to learn they would teach me themselves.

The most important thing that spirit went on to teach me (and always have drummed into me) is that spiritual development and the way of spirit is simple; it is simplicity in itself it is also very logical. Why must we complicate matters? I think it must be a human trait that it can't be good if it is too simple! But in truth it really is. It really is a case of learning how to open ourselves to all possibilities, to re-open the door of communication that we were born with and to open our minds to all possibilities, which for some is a difficult thing to do.

For many people most things are 'black and white', but there is that other area which many refuse to see, the greyer area in the middle. I often hear people say that if they can't see something with their own eyes it isn't really there, but there are so many things we just haven't learnt to see. Billions of people in this world believe in a God in their own religions but have they seen God? Mostly no, but it doesn't stop their belief. So why when we speak of spirit around and with us, do the same people who have that belief system suddenly change tack and say there are no such things as spirit or a spirit world?

Maybe it is a fear of having to accept that we are going home to the spirit world one day, as indeed that's where we came from, and that we may be accountable for our own actions here whilst on the earth. We are accountable for our actions whilst here, but our lives are a learning curve and a spiritual evolution for when we go back home.

I could never understand how people could believe that when we die that was the end of it. My mother used to say that to me as a child, *"When you're dead you're dead that's it"*, but I could never believe her. I always in my heart knew this wasn't the end of it and I always believed we went on to another place and that belief never left me. I found it quite sad that anyone could truly believe that when we leave this earthly body there was nothing more for us, it really didn't make sense to me at all! However, my mother did have a slight change of heart in later years as I became a Medium, I guess she either had to admit some truth in what I did or have to believe I was crazy! She chose to believe the former thankfully. Especially as time went on, I would talk about people she had known in the past, give her names of those I hadn't known and information I couldn't have known either, much to her surprise and to her sense of logic I might add, I found it somewhat amusing to watch her face drop!

I always remember the night my mother passed away from cancer, I had been at the hospital all night until the early hours of the morning when the nurses suggested I leave to get some rest with the assurance that they would call me if there was any change. I agreed as the hospital was only 10 minutes from my home. I hadn't been home more than an hour or so when I was dozing off and was disturbed by someone calling my name. I then saw my mother smiling and laughing, she was dancing around she said *"You were right kid! Look at me now"*. I knew then she had passed away. Within a few minutes the phone rang it was the hospital telling me I needed to come up right away, when I reached the hospital the nurse informed me of what I already knew. The best thing was that I knew my mother was happy and at last acknowledged what I had always told her; the spirit lives on.

On many occasions since then I have had numerous conversations with my mother, she visits me frequently, which is a great comfort to me and always has been, and I find myself so very lucky to be able to do so. Although I miss her physical presence, she is always there to comfort me and indeed make me laugh when I need her. But the best thing is I know that she is free from pain and is happy as are all of those in the spirit world.

Chapter 3

So many people often ask me do I know what it is like in the spirit world? The Afterlife. Well I can truthfully say that I have been given the wonderful gift of insight into that world, I have been taken there and been shown and indeed been given a glimpse of another dimension, it truly is a beautiful place to be. Well how could it not be when there is nothing but love in that world for each other and all living things, respect and kindness is what makes it truly special and a happy place to be.

There are 7 basic levels in the spirit dimension, and levels within levels that we are firstly as spiritual beings evolving to. Our lives on this earth are a learning curve for our progression, not only as human beings here on this planet but for our spiritual growth too, for our development for when we return home.

It is an ongoing process of learning, growing and achieving a higher level of spirituality ultimately, but if we truly listen to the inner self, our own spirit, we will achieve our goals much more quickly and in turn be more complete and content as human beings. The world would be much better, as we would all be more caring, loving and kinder to each other.

In recent years I have heard many people talking about an 'Awakening', a spiritual one of course, but also asking if this is really true that we are awakening spiritually. Well yes it is, we are going through a transition, a long awaited one I might add, which was preordained for us many, many years ago by the greater powers of the spirit world.

It all started in 2012, many had believed of course that this year was to mark the end of the world, well of course it wasn't but in another way it was the year to make a great change, the end of our world as we know it in many ways. It marked the 'Awakening', or the 'Ascension' is another term used for it, but it all meant one thing that we as human beings were to awaken our spirituality. To connect us to the spirit world to enable us to heighten our own abilities and to awaken us to the truth and reality that we are spirit, and we must realise and understand this to a greater degree.

How else will this world we live in change? We must become better people, we are not expected to be perfect of course but we need to think about how we treat people, how we react to people, and to take time for people to understand each other, our different cultures and way of life and be more accepting of each other. We are naturally good, we are born good, loving human beings but life can change our way of thinking, but the responsibility is ours. We are responsible for each other and especially responsible for our own deeds and actions. This responsibility goes further than our world too, we take that responsibility into the next life, for that in part is how we progress in the spirit world. We have many lessons to learn.

The spirit world is a very forgiving place, however if we choose to do the wrong thing continuously in this life on earth, we will inevitably have to accept the consequences of our actions when we go home to the spirit world. As I said we are here to learn and progress spiritually not just as human beings, but to evolve the spirit. Upon returning home all things are made clear to us, the wrongdoings, mistakes, the lack of compassion and learning whilst on the earth, all things become clearer to us as we have a greater knowledge within that becomes apparent when we become spirit.

However, the spirit world is truly a world of compassion, love and understanding where we will receive all these things in abundance, also forgiveness should we show remorse for the ill deeds we have done. Healing is an amazing thing and we will be given time to heal the spirit, for all wrongdoings on the earth cause pain and suffering to our own spirit.

Going home is the most natural thing for us all,

it is where we came from and return to when our earthly life comes to its end, but never fear the spirit world for it is truly a beautiful and wondrous place to be. We have no need for our physical bodies, our thoughts and processes return to a spiritual one as do our bodies, we become energy, a conscious higher thinking more powerful energy. We have no need for words as all communication is processed by transference of thought instantly, indeed we have no need for objects, houses or material things, not as we do in our earthly life as all needs are met for us. We can create such things should we feel a need to initially upon our return, as some do, but the realisation soon returns to us and the knowledge that we have no need for such things soon takes over and the desire for material things soon fades. We are then consumed with our purpose, the love there overrides all things and we are then ready to do the work necessary in the spirit world which indeed has purpose and reason. I have often been asked if we just float around in the spirit world doing nothing or just visit people on the earth, the answer to that is most emphatically NO; our purpose there is far more useful and rewarding.

Our work within the realms of spirit is indeed important, not just to the spirit world but to those on earth too. For spirit constantly work with us and help us when we call out for them, as often we do even those who say they have no belief in the afterlife or indeed any deity, at the worst times of their lives automatically call for help and guidance and raise their eyes to the heavens; haven't you…?

So many call out for their loved ones that have passed over asking for guidance, for them to show

us the way forward, to help with important decisions, and sometimes when we feel lost or in pain, we call for them or wish they were still here with us to help us - well they are. Our loved ones are only a thought away, it's a little like having a spiritual telephone, when we send out our thoughts to them our thoughts ring out like a telephone and they hear them and pick up for us. The only problem is so many haven't learnt to hear the voice on the other end of that 'phone', but believe me spirit will never be deterred, they will find a way to reach us and help us. But their purpose is not only about us, it is also the development and progression of themselves spiritually to grow and reach the higher levels within the spiritual dimension. This is achieved over a long period of time, not time as we know time as there is no need for time in their world. They do not live by it as we do, but it doesn't mean they have no perception of our time. They are aware of what time means to us and that our lives are governed by it, but the spirit world has no need for it, it is a man-made conception only.

Their work is to help each other and rise to greater heights and levels of spirituality. Many are designated to us here, to help us to do the same, to make our world a better and safer place to live and to help us to understand ourselves and our own spirituality. To bring that out in us and in turn bring love, peace and kindness to this earth. Indeed at this moment in time it is in great need of all these things.

Chapter 4

There is a great perception on this earth that all spirits are Angels or Guardian Angels. Indeed it is a lovely thought that we would like to believe that when our loved ones pass to the spirit world they become Angels. This is in fact not quite the case although there are indeed Angelic beings, but it is a status that has to be earned, yes even in the spirit world, so I would like to clarify and explain, as I have been enlightened myself by those in the world of spirit.

As I have mentioned before there are many levels in the spirit world but basically there are 7, the Angels and indeed Archangels come from the highest levels and are amazing beings that have evolved to the greatest heights. Indeed the Archangels are spiritual beings that have never walked the earth at any time and are therefore pure angelic & heavenly beings. They have great purpose in the spirit world and are the highest and most powerful of beings, next to God himself of course.

The Archangels have a greater task in overseeing the Earth plane and all other worlds, for our part on earth we were given the gift of free will and in many cases this has been our undoing, for such awful things that happen here such as wars and evil doings are borne of our own free will. It is easy for us to ask why God allows such awful and evil things to happen on the earth and doesn't intervene, which in turn causes many to question if God truly exists, but all this is created by mankind and is our responsibility to rectify and put right that which we have created.

If divine intervention were commonplace it removes our free will and our need to learn, grow and develop as the spiritual human beings that we truly are. That isn't to say that we do not receive divine intervention though for we do especially when things get truly bad, we ourselves call out through prayer for help here when in desperate situations and once we ask we often receive the help and guidance we need. Miracles do indeed happen.

Now back to the Archangels who oversee us and indeed try to keep us on the right path, on occasions they will intervene directly and personally if an occasion warrants them to but there is also an army of Angels ready to be deployed to help us when called upon. There are those in spirit also that help us in our daily lives, our families, Guides and Helpers are always at hand for us and will help when asked.

But most often than not we are helped by our families in spirit firstly, then if our needs are of a greater nature the angelic realms are called in to help, often we ourselves call out to God or the Archangels for help, and indeed all prayers are heard however loud or small the cry for help is made, it is heard by those nearest to us. If angelic intervention is needed and indeed warranted be sure that they will be there to help in whatever way is possible or necessary, our welfare is their greatest concern.

We also have to remember that we are here to learn and grow, spiritually, and as human beings although we sometimes think our pleas for help go unheard, this is not the case. Sometimes we have to learn to deal with situations ourselves in order to help us to grow for our personal development on this earth, however their help and guidance is always there for those who choose to listen. Having said that it is also possible if needed that spirit will intervene on our behalf too and often do in cases of emergency situations.

There are many reports throughout our history of people that have experienced divine intervention in many ways and had many amazing experiences that often cannot logically be explained, especially where lives have been saved in the most inexplicable ways. These truly are miracles and they come in so many ways, more happen on this earth than we care to acknowledge or accept unfortunately, but they are there for the eyes to see and the heart to feel, if only we would open both to them.

There have been many reports and indeed video footage has been captured of such events, but it is the norm of the human mind to question them, even when something happens in plain sight and is seen with our own eyes! Why do we still question and dismiss such amazing phenomena? Out of fear? Or is it because we fear other peoples' reactions to our stories and that we may get those knowing looks of disbelief? That we may be thought of as foolish or crazy? Well probably, but such things should be spoken of and shared for all truth should be shared to the accepting and the disbelieving. The seeds are sown in many ways.

It is definitely a time for sowing seeds here for it is the only way we can grow and move forward. I have found over many years of working as a Medium and sharing the knowledge I have learnt and experienced to others, it is a way forward for many people, an acceptance of another world, another dimension that we came from and will return home to one day is always, I believe, a source of comfort to many. Indeed in different ways to some, but none the less brings a feeling of acceptance, calm and positivity to so many. There is no greater feeling of knowing that we continue in another place after our physical body dies, to know that the loved ones we have lost are still there around us and waiting for us to go home when it is our time is a great comfort to us all.

That knowledge when it is accepted also brings a change to so many people, I have seen personalities change, peoples' desire to be a better person and become more caring and thoughtful of others, and that indeed is a wonderful thing to see and be a part of; albeit sometimes it is not easy and human nature is not naturally all forgiving, but it is something we need all to try hard to be.

I myself have had a few of these wondrous experiences in my life, spirit have saved my life on more than one occasion. At one time many years ago, I was very ill and bed bound with severe stomach pains, I thought at the time it could be my appendix, but was diagnosed with a kidney infection. This situation went on for two weeks until I could hardly move, I was pale and in pain with a swelling on my stomach, but still the doctor visiting me said it was just an infection.

One morning on waking up I heard a voice call out my name loud and clear, then I heard the voice tell me that I needed to get to hospital now otherwise I would die, needless to say I didn't argue! I was admitted to hospital and the next day was rushed to the operating theatre. I had an abscess on my appendix and bowel and it was seeping into my system causing septicaemia. The surgeon told me that one more day and I wouldn't have been here - I was a very lucky lady! It certainly wasn't my time to leave this earth and spirit made sure of that with the help of an amazing surgeon too!

So you see they can and do help us when needed and when we listen of course, if I hadn't heard that voice so clearly that day and acted upon it I wouldn't be here to tell the tale now.

Chapter 5

On my spiritual journey over these past 30 years or so I have encountered many people with a true desire to understand the truth and workings of spirit and the world we come from. I have always been led along a pathway to teach and help people to understand the truth about spirit and indeed ourselves, as we are spirit too, and more and more now in this day and age I do believe more people are looking and reaching out for an understanding. So many have a desire to understand such matters and often don't understand why the desire to learn more becomes stronger, but people are searching. First, we have to eliminate the fear.

So many do not understand that our loved ones who have left us and passed on to the wonderful world of spirit are still and always here for us, watch over us and always try to help us when we are in need, they love us unconditionally so why would they wish to harm us? They have only a desire to bring comfort and love to us all. We call upon them constantly asking for help and guidance as if they were still here, don't we? They come to us as always to try to help us.

Everything is not always rosy in families of course and many have suffered in the hands of family, and no matter how badly that person may have treated you whilst on this earth their personalities and understanding changes once in spirit, for we acquire a greater understanding there; a realisation of who we were and what we have done and then it is time to atone.

Many who seek messages from loved ones don't always understand that when someone comes through either in public demonstrations or in private readings that were in this kind of relationship before passing only wish to come and atone for their wrongdoings against us, to say sorry, sadly so many rebuke their efforts and have no desire to communicate with them and hold such negative feelings in their hearts for them, to those I would say, remember they are no longer that person and have moved on to a higher level of existence and knowing, and do not have those desires to hurt or inflict pain upon us anymore.

It is up to us to do the hardest thing there is to do in human nature and that is to forgive. As human beings it is necessary to learn to forgive although we never forget of course, but it is a part of our progression and development in this life to try to do so and that is the only way that we often find the peace inside that we truly need to move forward in life.

Our fears are of a world that we cannot see with our own eyes and also the stories of all things supernatural, things that 'go bump in the night'. So many films, books and through television are all things that cause us to fear spirit, of course with much there is a basis of truth about it, but the human imagination is an amazing thing and so much is sensationalised, we do indeed have a strange love of being scared witless!

However, it is time that we understood that yes, there are bad spirits out there, as there are human beings on the earth, but we need to understand that communication and connection especially with our loved ones in spirit is the most natural thing for us and indeed for them for they are always part of us and we are part of them. If we could only listen to our own spirituality we would realise this and also that there is no need to fear them.

Spirit of course can often get a little exuberant to say the least and can go overboard in their attempts to let us know they are here with us, especially when we have been talking to them, wishing they were still with us here and asking for advice and of course we get frustrated when we don't 'hear' from them. But, if you were to hear their voices out loud or if they were to materialise in front of us we would most definitely be scared! They have no desire to frighten us so will often show us they are there in usually more subtle ways.

I suspect many of you have experiences such things, the lights rising and falling, televisions, kettles, music systems etc being turned on or off randomly? All these things are very easy for spirit to do as they are indeed energy and can influence electricity easily, even mobile phones too. That in itself to some is a little scary but it is their way of showing us they are there. Also many have and do experience the sound of footsteps around the house, doors closing or opening such phenomena is common.

I have often been asked why spirit occurrences often happen at night when we are in bed? Well it is usually because you are at your most relaxed and especially your mind. If we ask for guidance from them that is the time we get our inspiration from them, it is usually the time before sleep when our minds are most at peace and have the most clarity, they can then inspire us with thoughts, help and guidance.

Our daily lives are often so busy in so many ways and our minds are constantly taken up with thoughts of life, work and family issues so it is very difficult at times to 'listen' to spirit, unless of course you have learnt how to open yourself and develop to a degree to allow them in freely.

That in itself is not always an easy task either, to learn to open ourselves to communication with our loved one's in spirit is indeed a long and frustrating task. To open our minds again, to open that doorway to another dimension is something that takes years of patience, dedication and a desire to do so, but well worth the time and effort!

However, for many on this earth it is now becoming easier and so many are finding they are having more and more spiritual experiences, we are indeed becoming more aware we just need now to learn to understand it and accept it. As I have mentioned before it is now a time of Awakening and developing spiritually, for how else can this world change for the better?

I have also found more recently (especially over the past few years) that so many people have a desire for an understanding and knowledge of the spirit world and indeed ourselves as we too are spirit. However with that desire comes sadly a fear, it's a case of "*I want to know but I'm afraid to know*"; but the desire to learn and understand is thankfully stronger in most people.

For doesn't knowledge enlighten us? With a greater knowledge of what was always referred to as the 'unknown', it no longer becomes the unknown and there is less fear, surely then it is better to understand and learn for fear is our greatest enemy and often holds us back in this life. So remember always ask the question not just of spirit, although they will indeed guide you to the answer if you are patient, but of those who have learnt to grow and understand, true Mediums that are truly guided by spirit to help, educate and give insight into that wonderful world.

There is a lot to take in and learn of course and maybe we will only learn that which we need to in this life to get us through on our pathway, but it is a never-ending learning and growing curve that we are going through, not just in our earthly life but in our evolution as human beings and as spirit. But if we ask there is always help and guidance for us on even our darkest days.

Chapter 6

Another question I am often asked is do evil spirits and demons exist? Well yes they do like anything in this world and the next where there is good there is bad, where there is love there is hate and so on. A great deal of the work I do now is what I would refer to as Clearances. You may have often heard the terms clearances, rescue and indeed other terms but these are very different things. Rescue work is simpler, this term relates to people that have passed away and have not allowed themselves to return to the spirit world, where we all need to go home to.

For many reasons they become earthbound. This could be that they are afraid to leave family in the belief that they cannot return to visit them, which is of course not the case - we can frequent the earth and our families whenever we choose to and are ready to. Others have a strong connection with their home and are not willing to give it up usually to someone else! In these instances we often hear about 'hauntings' not always of a positive nature of course!

Some are just afraid to let go and return home and do not wish to believe they have truly passed away and can be in denial. These cases are often helped to cross over by connecting and talking to them, explaining there is nothing to fear and no need to stay on the earth, once they have insight, they will pass over to the spirit world.

Some however decide that they have no desire to return home and decide they wish to stay in that other dimension where bad spirits reside, this would only be the case generally when a person too has led an evil life on this earth, these generally are not for 'rescuing' as they have no desire to be rescued sadly. So many reasons but the majority of us will cross over to the spirit world happily and willingly, thankfully.

Clearances are different altogether, there are entities that have not passed to the spirit world and entities that have resided in another dark dimension for an eternity. I wish I could say they don't exist but that would be foolish of me as I have encountered many and dealt with many, they prey on us and indeed our negativity and can cause many problems for us in this world, they thrive on evil deeds and destruction, but are more than happy to cause it themselves.

As we can be influenced by good we can also be influenced by evil, we all have a constant battle going on with that 'inner voice' urging us to think bad thoughts and do bad deeds, but mostly we fight it and allow the good in us to prevail and take over. Such entities can cause many negative reactions in us, cause us to be depressed, feel unwell, often cause us to lose sleep by waking us up constantly - there is nothing worse than sleep deprivation to lower our defences! In some cases can also cause physical harm, scratches, bruises etc.

These can also attach themselves to us, you may

have heard the term 'attachments' and they must be removed to allow us to return to our normal way of life. I know this may all sound somewhat far-fetched and many would say is not possible but I assure you it is and certainly since we have started Awakening spiritually these entities are far more active in our lives. They have no desire to lose control of us and are more determined to prevent us from growing spiritually to become better people and make a difference on this earth.

I used to be asked many years ago to help people that had activity in their homes, many who have been hurt physically and frightened in many ways by an unwanted entity, but this used to occur rarely maybe 4 or 5 times a year, sadly times have changed I am asked to do clearances on a daily basis often 4 or 5 times a week! Such is how it is changing and we must be aware and also ask for protection for ourselves and our families. I have encountered evil entities and seen demons, but I am truly grateful to the spirit world for giving me abilities to enable me to work with spirit of the highest realms and remove these entities.

I have also cleared many places not just houses; I have cleared schools, churches, leisure centres, outbuildings, office buildings, hotels, many different places in many different countries too around the world, where there are people they will follow. Please do not let this allow you to fear for there are so many that will never have such encounters in this life, but there are so many that do and once removed life can return to normal.

I have also sadly had to work with many children that have had problems with attachments such as these, children too are very open to spirit generally and on occasions have encounters like this which can change their personality, going from a loving well behaved child to the complete opposite almost overnight. Thankfully once the entity is removed they return back to behaving the way they were previously and almost instantly.

I have been fortunate over the years to have been allowed to grow and indeed progress to a stage where spirit have given me the abilities to work alongside them to remove such entities and demons from the earth. It is however an ongoing situation for they grow and amass, but I am also fortunate that I have no fear of such things, something I believe spirit have helped me with of course but I never have since the first time I did such a clearance and encountered and physically felt and saw such evil. It left no doubt whatsoever in my mind that these demonic influences are real. Much I have seen and experienced have been encounters enough for a good horror story! Who knows, maybe later…

What never ceases to amaze me is the closed mindedness of many practicing Mediums, Clairvoyants and Psychics those who will continually deny the existence of anything evil around us, I have heard many in denial and then tell a person going through an experience such as this to burn sage or 'smudge' their house to cleanse it! Really? I have no desire to be disrespectful to anyone's beliefs but sage or any other such practice in my experience has never removed a dark entity or demon, I have been contacted many a time following such practices to help as it hasn't worked and the 'activity' in the home has worsened after a day or two.

Logically how can burning a herb remove spirit? Can it isolate the good from the bad? If it did we would have no family in spirit around us either would we and that is something no one wants, to remove our loved ones in the spirit world. These entities are far stronger than any effects of any herbs or chant or such practice sadly, but it is in my belief a practice used out of desperation.

It is easier for some to say these entities do not exist than to accept it, some will do so as they have no idea of how to remove them or indeed any desire to encounter them, I truly don't blame them at all for the latter of course, but if they truly listen to their Guides and teachers who will speak the truth, it is a truth that we all need to have some understanding of and to not tell people that have had such bad experiences that it is in their imagination! For these encounters can be prolonged and painful, emotionally and physically and very draining on a family or indeed individuals. It is easier to put a label on people and call them crazy or insane than to accept the truth in many cases.

But as I have said before it is a time of Awakening for us all, a time of greater understanding of such things and an acceptance of all things, all I would say to you is to keep an open mind on all things spiritual. There are so many people in this world that have had so many encounters with evil spirits that it is something that cannot be ignored, so many are afraid to speak of such events for fear of another encounter, but I believe many are doing so more and more sometimes not understanding why entirely, but I believe it is a necessity to make people aware and to seek help so that these experiences can be shared to remove the fear and also in time clear the earth of such evil and negativity.

I do believe that knowledge is better than ignorance and we cannot bury our heads in the sand and hide from such matters that are going on all around us constantly. So how do we deal with negativity? With positivity of course, as we need to deal with hatred with love, with everything there is an opposite it is a fact of life and if we accept that then we need to accept that where there are spirit there is good, but there is also evil.

Love is the most powerful emotion of all and I do believe that it will always overcome hatred and evil, but it is hard isn't it to continually send out our love to all especially when there is so much evil on this earth, mostly created by mankind I might add, but we do attract what we send out, so it becomes a vicious circle if we send out bad thoughts or carry out deeds of hatred and evil, then is it not so that we would attract such things back upon ourselves?

Certainly we would attract spirit that are evil too and that then would enhance our mood and our situations, our own thought process would deteriorate too, leaving us in a very bad place indeed. Whilst in that 'place' is when those nasty entities are in their element and can prey upon us. Hard as it may be in many cases, as indeed we are only human after all, it is always beneficial to us to try to keep our thoughts on the positive, to try to forgive, to send out thoughts of love and positivity to the world we live in, that is what will change the world, that is what will make the difference and indeed we are ready for that!

So next time you are feeling angry with someone or just angry at the world we live in, stop, take a moment, take a breath and think of only positive thoughts even if it means diverting your thoughts to something past or present in your life that makes you smile, makes or made you feel happy, anything that helps to remove those negative thoughts and emotions, until those feelings of anger and negativity are gone. The power of positive thought is what will truly make a difference and indeed help you too, for those feelings are only more destructive and that none of us need in our lives.

It's a different world we live in these days for sure, it's busier, there is more stress, pressure of all natures certainly financially and emotionally, stronger desires and pressures to succeed but all too often we are trying to get there as fast as possible which causes more frustration and anger if we don't. It all brings on criticism from others, jealousy, envy, indeed all negative emotions which intensifies our energies but not in a good way. We need to slow down a little, take a rest, learn to relax again and mostly we need to learn to look at ourselves.

There are so many people that suffer from anxiety today especially the young and so many under that pressure to do well, that it causes negative emotions in them, so often we look at what is on the outside and completely forget that what is important in life is who we are on the inside, it is not so much what we achieve but how we achieve it! Time I think to step back and look at who we are not what we are.

I have met many young people searching for 'something', not religion necessarily, but deep down inside have a need to fulfil a purpose and gain an understanding of life not just the materialistic things of life but a spiritual understanding. As I said before, we are spirit ourselves and I believe that we are being empowered by spirit to awaken our own spirituality. There is of course a reason for this, for as we awaken, and many young people are, and many children are being born that are more spiritually advanced, they will in time change the world we live in and bring it together.

I do not see spirituality as a religion, I see it as a way of life, something positive. I have seen many people come to Centres all over and yes they are attracted by the thought of being able to speak to loved ones, to be guided by them, to be given hope by them, for all that spirit give us is positive, but it often has an effect on them and can even change their perspective on life and also in how they treat other people. That indeed is a wonderful thing to see, to see growth in not only young people but people of all ages.

Don't get me wrong, I have no intention of 'preaching' to anyone, as I said for me it is not a religion in the conventional sense, spirit only have a desire to show us the truth, to give us positivity and to guide us in our lives in the best possible way, but to be the best we can possible be. They will never tell us what to do but if we ask for their help they will guide us on our pathway, the decisions are up to us and they will never take away our free will.

Chapter 7

Every day I turn on the television and look at the news, sadly all I seem to see these days is a world in chaos, more and more stories of death, murder and atrocities, terrorist attacks, more and more young people committing crimes and suicide. It breaks my heart to see this world in such a bad way as it does so many of us. However I am still a firm believer that there is much more good in this world; it seems that lately most of that which is reported is on the negative side. It does seem though that there are so many more evil doings happening of late doesn't it?

It would also serve that if there are more and more evil spirits & demons attacking the world it could easily trip many over the edge to commit such evil crimes. I am not saying that is the root cause of people's actions as that would be wrong and simply not true, as human beings we are more than capable of doing such things ourselves, but with influence it could trip many over the edge to do something they would not have necessarily done; maybe we need to keep an open mind and be a little more vigilant and aware of those around us and seek help for those in need too.

I have had many experiences in my life and none more so than now of personality changes in people that have acquired an attachment. Many will become moody, depressed, angrier than usual or even do many things out of character for them and become erratic. Usually this starts after some kind of activity in the home. Especially with children I have had many cases where a child may have a new 'friend' that appears as a child, which of course isn't, but can lull us into a false sense of security believing our child has a new 'invisible friend'. Such entities will not stay in that form for too long, they are too arrogant for that, just long enough to begin to affect a child's mind, goading them to be naughty and do bad things.

On the other hand often they will plague a home, a child that is sensitive to spirit, and most are, can be scared by them often being woken in the night and many seeing what is often described by them as seeing 'the nasty man or woman' in their bedrooms or indeed around the house. These entities can also infiltrate their dreams too causing nightmares. However on the positive side once removed a child will go back to normality almost instantly.

The same can be said of adults too of course and sometimes their experiences can be those you would only imagine in horror films, apart from attacking and changing a person's personality they can physically attack them too. I remember many cases such as this, one in particular comes to mind where a woman with a young family had been experiencing physical activity for at least five years. It became so bad that she had initially decided to move but what many do not realise is that even if you move the entity will go with you for they are much more interested in you than a house!

The family had had so much happening to them, furniture would move on its own, and I mean heavy furniture, the sofa would often start to shake especially when the children sat on it, doors would slam shut and the mother would wake with bruises and scratches on her body, it was endless and horrifying for the whole family. Once the entities were removed, immediately peace was restored in the house and thankfully no such experience has occurred again to my knowledge.

I have spoken to so many over the years that have had similar and some worse experiences and it can indeed be terrifying to experience, it doesn't just happen in horror stories or films; in fact many a story is based on such encounters in real life. I have had many come to me that have experienced bruising and scratches that have appeared on their bodies without explanation but always there is other activity that occurs as well.

Another case of physical harm was with a lady that contacted me, her son had been visited by a young man in spirit as he regularly spoke of him, it seems they became great friends over time. The boy could clearly see his spirit friend but suddenly it changed, the boy became naughtier and more disrespectful, something he had never done before, even at school his teachers had noticed a change in him and his ability to study and concentrate at school.

I was asked to visit after the lady had had a particularly bad encounter with her son's new friend. She had been in her kitchen and was telling her son off for being disobedient and he had hidden in a cupboard, she was telling him to come out and as she touched his arm, she suddenly felt something grab her. She described it as an energy that seemed to grab her stomach, she was lifted off the floor carried out of the kitchen into the hall and thrown down the hallway.

Unfortunately the force was such that as she

landed putting her hands out to break her fall, she broke both wrists! It was after this that she decided she needed help. I visited the house and removed the spirit. Her son's behaviour changed almost immediately without his friend to influence him and even his school commented to her that he was his old self again thankfully, although in this case it was not a demonic entity at fault but it was a rather naughty one that hadn't realised his own strength!

Many such occurrences can also be a cry for help from a spirit, so many buildings have 'hauntings', these are usually spirit that have attached to a property. It can be one that they lived in when they were alive, these cases are usually those that need help to cross over into the spirit world. There are many reasons why some don't and linger in a place that they were familiar with, sometimes it's a fear of letting go, sometimes it's a connection with those that may still reside there and sometimes it's just plain devilment that they wish to cause mayhem!

I have cleared many houses, schools, hotels, shops, even outbuildings of such spirit, many of which have a tendency to scare those in the property for in many cases we are quite easily scared or unnerved by such happenings, especially when we cannot physically see the perpetrator.

I remember when my daughter was at her primary school, I was called in to investigate some minor disturbances, which had tended to frighten the teachers more than the children to be honest, anyway one instance was that a teacher had gone behind the stage to get some paper which was stacked on shelving, as she walked in the paper began to fly off the shelves, also a cupboard began opening and closing, needless to say she didn't stay and ran out somewhat ashen!

The school had also had instances in the girl's toilets too with toilets flushing, taps being turned on and left on, usually happening when a child was in there, I suspect just trying to get attention and be noticed! However one day my daughter was in the toilet and these things started happening, she told me that when she came out of the cubicle there was a young girl standing there, my daughter realised she was spirit and stopped to speak to her. The child told her she was lonely and did it so that someone would talk to her, my daughter then told her that she needn't be lonely and that she could come home with her - this was in time to become a frequent thing!

I spent a short time at the school helping another young spirit there to go home to the spirit world, but also ended up with a spiritual addition to the family! The child in question was helped to the spirit world but would often pop back to say hello to my daughter.

For my part in this my job is to encounter all spirit, lost souls or otherwise, and to confront such entities - from just nasty spirits to demons, I have seen them all. I am fortunate to work with

Archangels to remove such creatures and have been given abilities to dispel them thankfully. It has taken many years of development and dedication to achieve this but I do believe it is one of the reasons that I am here in this life and at this time. I am not alone of course but for my part I work alone with spirit and as I said before I have no fear of such things, for which I am sure has come with me from past lives and also from the influence of the most amazing spirit. There are so many stories to tell of such experiences, but I do not want you to think it is all about such things, but it is important that we are aware that all things are possible in this life, but there is so much more good that can be experienced and learnt from the spirit world which far outweighs the bad.

We have a need now to try our hardest to be positive for as I have said positivity brings with it positive things not just for ourselves but for the world, we often underestimate the power we have within us and just how effective it can be. If more would send out those thoughts to the world we could change it.

Sadly so many at this time think more negative thoughts and thoughts of a more selfish nature, but that is human, we have to try harder to send kinder, nicer thoughts out to make a difference. It is strange in some ways that only when we have some kind of major disaster that touches us so deeply do we turn to prayer for those in need, our hearts go out to those that have and are suffering, and most undcrestimate how much that does help but if we could do that on a more regular basis? Well it could be immense and turn the world around.

We all spend so much of our daily lives just trying to get through each day such is the life we lead today and often don't have time to take a few minutes out for ourselves, to sit and contemplate, to relax, to send out positive thoughts to the world and all those in need and to ask for help for ourselves too which is important. If we are not in a good frame of mind it is even more difficult to send healing and positivity to others.

So stop, take a few moments to think, to heal yourself and the world and I guarantee it will help in many, many ways, it will often also bring you clarity.

Chapter 8

It is not all negativity though that is for sure, there is such an overwhelming positivity to working for spirit in every way. One of the things I truly love about my work is that it truly can help people in so many ways, whether it is to bring comfort for those who have lost loved ones or to bring evidence that we do continue on into another form and life, we never die. The body may give up on us eventually or for whatever reason but the spirit lives on in all its glory.

To truly give evidence of such survival brings about another thought process to many people, we are conditioned from the past and out of people's fear of what we cannot see cannot exist. So to be able help a person to open the parts of the human mind to understand that there is indeed so much we do not understand and that there is more to us than just a physical body can be truly life changing. Comfort is one of the first and most profound things to be able to give someone who is grieving, once a person accepts and understands the truth the healing begins. Then comes the wonderful feeling of knowing that our loved ones are so close to us and watching over us always ready to help and listen and guide us forward in our lives, it can never replace the fact that we can no longer physically touch or hug that person, but it brings great comfort to know that they are still there even if in another form.

However when we open ourselves to the concept that we are not alone we can truly feel the touch and love that spirit have for us, and that never dies or fades but will only grow stronger. I believe many people still talk to those that have passed, we still chat to them asking for guidance and help in our lives just as we did when they were here with us and that is normal, the problem comes then for many when they do not hear a response or believe they cannot hear us, this is not the case, they hear us loud and clearly.

We then become frustrated not just with those in spirit but with ourselves too, I am often asked *"Why can't I hear them?", "If you can, why can't I?"*. The answer is simple, we have to learn to hear them, to open the parts of our minds that have been closed since our childhood, for children it is a natural thing to see and hear spirit many just as they see those living around them, but as we grow older we have a tendency to close ourselves down. This is often through fear, other people's opinions and life generally, so we have to re-learn how to open ourselves again. This of course will take a lot of patience and perseverance. Any Medium will tell you that it takes a good many years to develop these abilities again, to open yourself to spirit once more and indeed a great deal of patience too!

But what I need to explain is that spirit will never intentionally scare us or put fear into us and that is one reason why we don't often hear that disembodied voice talking to us, not from our loved ones especially, they will be more gentle with us and this they can more easily do by inspirational thoughts.

So if you need their help ask away, but then leave it, the more you try to 'hear' them you will block them for if our mind is too 'busy' they cannot get through to us, but remember spirit will guide us but not tell us what to do in our lives as we have free will and they cannot take that away from us.

There are many decisions we have to make for ourselves, but they will certainly help us to get on the right path for us at that time. More often than not we ask, then at the most random time, usually when we are more relaxed and our mind is not troubled the answer and thought will be planted firmly in our head. I often refer to these moments as 'light bulb moments', we all have had those, when the answer pops into our head when least expected with cries of *"Why didn't I think of that before!"*. Little do we realise that it is often spirit answering our call for help, they are truly amazing.

Don't get me wrong though if needed spirit can call out to us loud and clear if really necessary and if a situation calls for it or sometimes it may just be to get our attention, but generally they have no desire to scare us. If those that have passed to spirit that loved us whilst alive why would they want to scare us or cause fear when they have passed over? The love they have for us intensifies and doesn't change.

We spend so much time asking for them to show us they are with us still or talking to them that sometimes they feel it necessary to let us know hopefully and usually by more subtle means, the most common ways are by fluctuating our lights in the home, turning on or off kettles, tv's, stereo systems and such things. These things are simple tasks for them as they can easily control electricity, even mobile phones if need be as spirit are energy.

Objects moving or indeed disappearing are also

common and disappearing items are very common amongst spirit children who like to play with us and get our attention, however they usually forget to replace the items… until reminded of course!

Spirit are also very good at bringing us smells, out of the blue you can have a strong sense of a particular smell almost instantaneously, it could be perfume or aftershave, of course one that our loved one's would have used, cigarette smoke if they were a smoker when here, they can bring us any related smell that will remind us of them it is another way of letting us know they are here with us.

They can of course touch us too and this has often been described as a feeling of cobwebs on the face or a brush against the skin. I'm not saying that every sensation we feel is spirit but it usually occurs when we have been thinking of them or talking to them, they will acknowledge they are here. They have however been known to be more direct of course and many have felt a definite poke or more forceful touch, just to make sure we are aware of them!

Animals visit us too which is a comforting thought also for many people and they too can make their presence felt, by touch, smell, or any other sensation, a dog may have been prone to jumping on your bed whilst alive and may continue to do so after it's passing, many have felt as if something had jumped on their bed and can feel the pressure of weight on the bed too. This can also happen with people that have passed for they will often come and sit with us, but animals in particular will show us in whatever way they can, also you may feel something leaning against your legs, especially if the animal was prone to doing so in life, it is to remind us and let us know they are there.

Another common instance is that of our other animals in the house will suddenly react to something you cannot see, but it will look as if it is listening or sometimes bark or whine when another spirit animal is present or a person is present. Animals can see spirit in all forms and are very aware. It is also an indication of a visitor that is not so pleasant that an animal will react very strongly as it will not be happy with the energy that is there, they may cower, raise their hackles and growl, hiss or react strongly to an 'intruder' in the same way it would with a human or animal intruder, only to settle when they have left. It is such a comfort to know that the pets we loved so dearly are still with us too, again they come only with love and to comfort us when we are in need, for they too are spirit and live on.

It is important that in this life we understand that spirit are not to be feared, for those that have loved us always will continue to love us forever, to be close to us when we need them to comfort and console us, we just need to remember that they are not gone just moved on to another dimension and another form, but the consciousness is still there and is amplified greatly. One day we will all meet again in that world. Our loved ones are there to meet us when it is time to go home and to help us to understand what is happening and to show us the way home too.

There are many cases of when a person is going through a prolonged illness, especially a terminal one, they will talk of seeing someone close to them that has already passed, we dismiss it as 'imaginary' or ramblings caused by illness, but in truth it is usually absolutely true and very real. For sometimes our family will come to prepare us and to let us know that we will see them again, it makes the transition from the earthly world to the spirit world so much easier and the most important thing of all is that it takes away any fear of dying and that is important for all of us.

So many people have such a fear of dying, if only we could all understand that we shall not die, we shed the physical body but we move on to a greater consciousness when we go home, for it is truly where we came from and inevitable that we return one day. No one likes to think of leaving our families behind and that as human beings is the hardest thing for us, not just the leaving them, but it is also the hardest thing to have someone close to us leave, to not be able to feel and touch someone again. But if we open our heart and mind believe me you will 'feel' them again, you can feel the love that will always surround you, the gentle touch of them and that feeling of love they bring us can be overwhelming.

I find it sad that so many people say that when you are dead that is it, there is nothing more, I have never been able to believe that or would want to believe it and if we allowed ourselves to open up to a spiritual existence, which I do believe we all have the knowledge of deep inside us, for we are spirit, and allow ourselves to believe and connect with it, there would be no more fear.

I have found over many years once people believe and understand, it changes them, to become a better person, or at least to try. It is a knowing that we continue on that gives us a desire to be better for we go to another place and therefore maybe our deeds done here may have a reflection on us when we get there. It makes us think more of what we do now and that has to be good.

Chapter 9

There are many people that ask if I believe in 'fate', are our lives predestined, is our pathway one that cannot be changed? Well, in some aspects we have lessons to be learned so we need to go through some experiences in this life to allow us to grow and to learn and to hopefully evolve spiritually and as human beings. But I do not believe our lives are set in 'concrete', we have been given free will on this earth and we have the right to use it of course, but often we find that if we stray from a particular course in life then we find ourselves back on that same or similar pathway. For me, I have learnt that it is better to follow its course and learn the lessons we need to learn to enable us to move forward.

Once the lesson is learnt, good or bad, we need to allow ourselves to move on and accept that this particular time in our lives was a lesson and once learnt will enable us to move forward with a greater awareness, knowledge and hopefully compassion. If we allow ourselves to recognise these events in our lives we will move on more quickly as opposed to allowing ourselves to wallow or be held back and then leave ourselves in danger of repeating our past mistakes or allow others to continue to treat us badly or unkindly.

All of life is knowledge, all of our experiences are growth we just need to understand and recognise that, then we can move forward a stronger, wiser person. Positivity is key even though your experiences are difficult, painful and hard, but not all our experiences in life are created by spirit of course, no, so much we create ourselves or are created by others and the problem is we do not listen to our inner self, to our own spirit that can lead us out of such situations that we place ourselves in or are indeed put in. So often we ask for help from those we pray to but forget to listen.

There is always help from spirit when we ask for

it, we just need to learn how to accept it and to hear it, but of course it doesn't come in the conventional way, we need to learn to open our minds and hearts to them, to not search for the answer immediately but to relax, open the mind and the answer or help will come by way of inspiration more often than not. Listen and you will find the way forward.

It is also about trust too, it is hard to learn to trust spirit isn't it, to trust in something or someone we cannot see is very difficult for us humans but that is something that has to be learnt. We find it hard to trust in ourselves and each other but to place our trust in them takes a lot of time and patience and indeed belief. I have come across so many people that find it hard to believe that another world exists after we leave this one, I have been taunted and jibed at saying *"Prove it"* - there are ways of course but a person has to be receptive to it.

Surely by listening to a Mediums' words during a reading or demonstration, a total stranger to you that can convey characteristics or description of a loved one that has passed, the knowing of what is happening in your life at that time, your needs and to give you guidance, to give you names of those that are no longer with you; we are not mind readers, that is not possible. I have also heard of people saying that we have researched them... Really? To do that you would need so much information from someone, full name, address, date of birth etc; this would take days and hours of time and what for? Would you give out that kind of information? I certainly wouldn't.

I for one and so many Mediums would have neither the time nor patience for such things, in fact the less we know of a person makes it easier to keep the mind open and clear to enable communication to be possible. Also when doing public demonstrations and travelling to different areas with anything from 30 to 50 and upwards of people in attendance? Impossibility!

There are millions of people all over the world that believe in God and none of us can prove that beyond a doubt, but there is belief and faith, so why should it be so easy for those to question and condemn that the spirit world exists? Fear maybe? But in this world today there are many, many people that have encountered such spiritual experiences that so many claim are lies and attention seeking practices, some are of course but so many aren't. Is it just a fear of acceptance that it does exist? Or that we would have to open our minds to a reality beyond our comprehension, beyond what we see with our own eyes?

As we move closer to spirit at this time and they move closer to us and are making us more aware they are there, I do believe that opinions are changing slowly, minds are becoming more open, the fear is waning. In time I also believe that the belief and acceptance will come, we are growing spiritually now and it is as it should be, how we are meant to be, and it is the only way the world will become a better place to live in and for us to treat each other with love, respect and acceptance. Sadly this could take some time yet but I believe we are on the pathway now. We can overcome the evil and hatred that surrounds us in this world but it can only be fought against with love, and that we all have in abundance we just need to remember to send it out to others and to the world and the earth itself to heal all living things.

I do believe that we all have lessons to learn during our time on this earth and very important ones too, although I doubt sometimes we see that ourselves. I also believe that so many are here to make a difference to the world too, those that have a purpose, to make a change for the better, to do or speak out to bring positive change for us. Where there are negatives there will always be the positives and that applies to people as well as practices. We have had so many such amazing people through history that have brought positive change to situations, also many evil and bad that have brought negativity worldwide, but there is always and always has been the good that has come to defeat the evil. We truly are strong in adversity and will always pull together, to fight evil deeds and to bring about positive change. To stand together in unity and to pull together in times of tragedy it is in our nature and will always be so.

What is difficult for many to understand is that we are spirit too, our spirit resides within us we just need to learn how to 'tap' into it to listen to that inner 'voice' that comes from within. We all have two sides to us, one that is dark and one that is light, for me the light comes from the spirit within that is good and positive and keeps us from doing bad things, our conscience. But we also have a greater knowledge inside us that many haven't yet learnt to tap into, a greater understanding.

The dark is a human side, the part that makes us

think bad thoughts or want to do bad things, some will sadly allow that side to take over of course, but most of us will always allow the light to push through which then makes us do the right thing. Having a few bad thoughts just makes us human and is normal at times for we are not perfect of course, but to allow our inner light to shine is what makes us truly who we are. It is what makes us complete as a person, that the light is allowed to shine, that we do connect with our own spirit too which keeps us grounded and on the right pathway. Once we learn to allow our inner self to shine forward, we not only become better people but it brings with it a greater understanding of all things, a greater awareness of life and each other and that is what we need here now.

The knowledge we have deep within us is truly extensive, for many years I have worked and developed my spiritual abilities especially when it comes to educating people in matters of spirit and the spirit world. So many over the years that I have connected to and spoken to in my capacity as a Medium and teacher have asked so many questions, questions that I believe we have all thought of and wanted to ask and so far I have always been able to give them an answer. That is partly to do with a spiritual connection which enables me to connect with spirit to gain an answer but also over the years I have found the answer is just there!

I was talking with a number of people one evening and they were all asking questions about spirit and the spirit world, some questions I had already heard before of course and having that knowledge myself now was able to answer, however a number of other questions arose too which were intriguing, thankfully I answered them and thought to myself how wonderful that my Guides can give me these answers and I thanked them for that. However the next thing I heard was *"No we didn't give you the answer you gave it yourself"*. Well I was a little perplexed,

I asked *"How?"*. My reply was that the answers had come from within me, my own spirit that knew the answers to these questions, I had now begun to learn to connect with my own spirit. Well I was amazed to say the least! But when I contemplated this it came to me, we all have a greater knowledge within us, our spirit has been around a long time, far longer than this body it inhabits has been, and so it stands to reason that there must be a greater knowledge within us when we have had other lives too on this earth.

There then comes an amalgamation of knowledge within, but it takes a very long time to accept this and in turn learn to open ourselves and connect with our inner self, but it does show that all things are possible when you open yourself to that possibility. We have so much to learn and so much to give to this world so allow yourself that open mindedness and allow yourself to be open to all possibilities, for there is far more to each of us than we ever realise is possible.

Chapter 10

I do believe however that many people would love to be able to communicate with our loved ones in the spirit world themselves and I am often asked *"How can you and I can't?"*. Well, as I have previously mentioned we all have an ability, we are all 'Psychic' and are born that way, but often life itself or the influence of others 'shut us down' over time and of course, fear. But I like many others and many now who are learning to open themselves again are learning how to re-open that doorway of the mind to spirit and what an amazing journey that can be. I have been teaching development to people for over 27 years, even those who thought they would never be able to connect have with time, perseverance and patience found that some communication is possible, but how that develops is mainly down to the individual.

I also believe that in some the desire to develop

and abilities are stronger but if you have that dedication the doors will be opened to you. As I mentioned before we are all 'Psychic' but there is a difference between the psychic and the spiritual levels that we can learn to attain. For me there is no stronger link than that of a spiritual connection, it is of a higher level and does take a little longer to learn to attain, but is truly worth the time and effort it needs to reach those levels.

It is hard for many that strive to learn to connect I cannot lie, so many may say it is easy but truly it is not. It takes a number of years to develop your abilities to a spiritual level. I hear so many times of courses being run promising a 6 week intensive course to connect you with spirit, this is not realistically possible and indeed is misleading to many who have a true desire to learn, there is no 'quick fix' here unfortunately.

There are many more people coming to spiritual centres and churches, I am often told that some people have no real idea of why they came but just felt an urge to do so. I believe it is spirit pointing us in the right direction, either because we need evidence of life after life, we need guidance, help or an understanding and hopefully they will leave having a greater understanding or acceptance of spiritual matters. The greatest gift from such visits is that it can often take away that fear of the 'unknown'. I also believe that spirit are guiding us to find the truth to give us comfort and hope but also a belief. It is time for us to change and the fastest way for that to happen is to raise our spirituality within ourselves to help us to realise what is truly important on this earth. We have a great capacity to love as human beings, but we also have a capacity to hate which is truly a negative pathway. I have often found over the years that those who begin to understand true spirituality do become better people and suppress desires of negativity and hatred.

We are born with only the ability to love and be

nurtured, if we could maintain that then the world would be an amazing place to live, but I live in hope and the knowledge that love truly does overcome hatred and there are far more people that have love within them than hate. The rest just need a reminder of who we truly are. There is no greater power or human capacity than our ability to love and forgive and that I believe is why spirit are coming ever closer to us to remind us of that ability and power within us.

So how do we open those doors to connect with spirit? Well as I said it isn't easy but it is possible. It's about taking time out to sit quietly sometimes to relax the mind and open your mind to all things, if you constantly sit thinking *"Well, I'm asking but not getting anything back"*, then you won't. Try to sit quietly and clear your mind ask your loved ones to come close, if you need help from them or guidance then ask but do not expect a voice to boom out telling you what to do! They are not in the business of scaring the life out of us and that is what would happen if they did, so, ask your question then just relax enjoy the peace and quiet and at some stage they will give you your answer.

Just remember they cannot give you material things, but hope, guidance and healing they can. But it often comes when you are not searching, when the mind is at its least busy. If your mind is racing of the thoughts and problems of everyday life they cannot get through to us easily, we block the thoughts and inspiration that they do come to give us. They never deny us but we must learn to accept how they can communicate with us without scaring the life out of us!

On the other hand they are very capable of calling and speaking out loud to us too. Over the years I have often heard that disembodied voice call to me, usually because I wasn't taking notice of them when they wanted to communicate with me and yes it made me jump! Many have reported voices calling out to them and even spirit can get a little frustrated at times and feel the need to make themselves heard. More often than not it is those that are closest to us, our family and loved ones, but sometimes just some that are drawn to us. For the thoughts and pleas we send out to the spirit world are indeed heard by many.

I remember when my daughter was young I would often be woken by hearing a voice calling *"Mummy"*, I would get up and go to her bedroom only to find her sound asleep, return to bed and hear it again. This went on for a few days until I stopped and said out loud *"Ok that's enough"*, after asking who it was calling me I heard the giggling of small children. Not mine I hasten to add but spirit children that had taken to visiting my home frequently. It didn't take us long to come to the understanding that they are more than welcome to be there and visit on the condition that they do not wake me up! They still visit my home now many years later and indeed spent a great deal of time with my daughter as she was growing up and to this day visit her frequently.

So if you are disturbed in this way at any time remember to tell them that it is not acceptable and to tell them to go away if you are uncomfortable with their visits, this also applies to all spirit not just children of course. Most of the visitations we have are by those who have no desire to harm us but do get a little over-zealous in trying to get our attention. Of course it's not just the voices we hear that gain our attention, more often than not spirit will try to get us to notice them mostly in our homes, as I previously mentioned, by playing with your lights, making them fluctuate up and down is very common, also turning on electrical goods, they are very good at doing this and it certainly gets our attention! They are also very adept at moving things too and hiding them. Usually these things more often happen when we have been thinking of them and talking to them it is another way of them showing us they are there.

If you do encounter such experiences and it

makes you feel uncomfortable or afraid then tell them, after all these are your family and friends and those closest to you that are trying to let you know they are around you, ask them to step back, to stop, but acknowledge them; often that is all they are trying to tell you, that they are there for you they are listening to you. They have no desire to scare you or indeed make you feel uncomfortable but we ask for their help and guidance and it is their way of letting you know they have heard you and are there for you to help in any way they can.

Aren't we the strangest? We call out to those who have passed for the help, guidance and support which they gave us when they were here with us on this earth, but as soon as they try to let us know they are still with us in the only ways they can, we panic and are afraid! They will always try to be gentle with us but there are only so many ways they can let us know they hear us, they will always use the more subtle ways as opposed to materialising or speaking directly out loud to us as that would cause even more distress and fear in us.

So next time you ask for their help expect to be given a sign in some way as usually they will, especially when we are at our lowest ebb they will be with us and try to help us for they feel our pain and will do anything they can possibly do to help ease our suffering, physically and emotionally. The love they had for us on the earth never dies it continues even stronger when they go home, it is unconditional and more intense than even we can comprehend, but it is true love and that is a truly beautiful thing.

As a Medium I can truly say it is one of the most amazing feelings when bringing a loved one in spirit through for someone, the feelings are incredible especially the feeling of love that comes through it can be quite intense but oh, such a wonderful feeling to be able to feel their love for you which is even stronger than before it can be quite breath-taking, literally, and also a very emotional one too. To be able to give that and indeed all their feelings and words to their loved one here is for me the greatest gift. Becoming a Medium is truly for me, a gift, to be able to bring people and spirit together again is a wonderful thing.

However it does come with a great deal of responsibility, I do believe it should too and should only be used to help people in need and also to prove that life does not end when the physical body passes away. It should be used to bring peace and comfort to all, but all too often it can be abused, and where there is money to be made it does and has attracted many charlatans, those who claim to be Mediums, Clairvoyants, Psychics and are very clever at asking questions to obtain responses and information from you. This saddens me of course but as in all aspects of life and practices there are people that will lie and con you to obtain your money. So be careful, be mindful and often the best way is to find a Medium is one that is recommended to you by others as opposed to an advert in your local paper, or go to your local spiritualist Church or Centre they will help you.

Chapter 11

I have taught many people to develop their abilities over the years and many who are Mediums today, the one thing I have always stressed to them is to give the evidence and words they receive directly, to trust spirit, and to not ask questions as this can often cause mistrust between the reader and the client. Once the connection between the Medium and spirit is stronger the information you receive will flow with greater clarity therefore there is no need to dispute or question the information you receive.

There is a fine line when developing one's spiritual abilities to allow the mind to interfere with spirit communication, to allow yourself to try to analyse the images, feelings and words you receive, which is human, but it doesn't work as then the message becomes your interpretation and not spirits words and can become frustrating to both parties and indeed very confusing.

This is one of the reasons it takes a long time to develop these abilities, it is not an easy thing to do to allow yourself to clear your mind completely to allow the thoughts, words and images of spirit to enter the mind with clarity. As human beings we have tendency to question spirit, *"I don't understand what you mean"* - truthfully, you don't have to and the likelihood is you won't understand the messages you are giving, for they are not your messages to understand. They are meant for the recipient and as long as they understand is all that matters.

However as I said it is not an easy thing to do but is a necessity to enable you become the channel for spirit that you need to become, to enable you to pass on those messages from loved ones in spirit.

Giving messages are not the only way we use our abilities, there is actually a greater scope of Mediumistic abilities we can learn to use and tap into, of course they all involve the connection to spirit but can be used in different ways.

One of the lesser spoken of ways is to help solve crime and especially murders, however a Medium's input is not evidence allowed in a courtroom of course, but it has been used time and time again by many open-minded police officers to point them in the right direction so to speak and enable them to find a culprit. This is of course done by connecting to the spirit of the departed or their family in spirit but it is possible and has been going on for many many years, it is just one of the unspoken practices that is used, sadly not used as frequently as it could be.

We have truly moved forward over the last decades in the ways we approach and accept such things but we still have a long way to go. With the help of Mediums time and financial implications could be eased too, although not always as quickly as we would like, it can have a positive effect on investigations and in some cases save lives too.

One of the lesser known secrets of the second world war were the use of Mediums to track and find enemy ships and such like, you may ask why would spirit do such things? Well, they will always be on the side of truth, justice and good and will help us to fight evil in all forms where necessary.

As I said before there are a number of ways that mediumistic abilities can be used, often it is called upon to find a missing person, not just those that have passed away, in these instances a connection can be made either by connecting with their loved ones in the spirit world or a connection can be made by visiting an area, the persons home or even personal items that belong to them, this can establish a link and ultimately it will be spirit that will help along the pathway to locating someone.

Sometimes however the information can come in the form of a jigsaw puzzle, pieces of information given to the Medium that will need to be pieced together. This will also depend on a person's connection and of course we are all human and slight errors can be made, but generally it comes and can be pieced together, sadly though often in a sceptical world it isn't always believed by those searching, and can be disregarded all too quickly, only to be found to be true at some later date.

Don't get me wrong we all know that there are many that would claim to be Psychics or Mediums that will offer false information, it is the nature of humanity in some cases, but I have found that the information a true Psychic or Medium would offer will always have a 'trigger', information that cannot be denied and that should allow the recipient confirmation of the rest of the information provided. Most that is given is usually very easy to check out, and if it proves helpful? Then surely it is worth the time to listen. More to gain than lose if it proves useful.

One of the most wonderful forms of spiritual connection and abilities is that of Healing, many who develop their connections are also healers, of course this has become more popular over the years and many have turned to healers for help either through spiritual Healing, Reiki and so many other forms that have grown over the years. I personally am a spiritual Healer I have found, for me, that it is the simplest form of healing to learn and to practice and I am all for simplicity! There is much controversy over healing often dubbed as 'faith healing' but it is not, it is about becoming a channel for spirit to transfer their amazing abilities to heal through you and this also has to be learnt just as much as it has to be learnt to communicate.

Healers often grow, the energy can grow stronger as you progress these abilities. I have experienced and seen so many amazing things over the years, I have seen tumours shrunk enough to allow surgery and patients cured from that surgery, I have known those unable to conceive easily to conceive, but healing is not only for the physical conditions but also for the emotional too, it can reduce stress, anxiety and many other symptoms. I am not saying that healing will always cure the body or mind but it goes a long way to helping to ease that burden of pain and suffering.

As with all things there are no guarantees with healing but it can certainly help in so many ways, and yes who knows in some healing can assist with a cure, I truly believe that all things are possible and what is meant to be will be. So when you go to a healer go with an open mind but go with the ability to let yourself feel the benefits, great or small, but one thing is for sure you will leave with a greater sense of well-being.

Trance communication is another way to use such a connection, however I would not advise anyone to attempt a trance state unless they were more spiritually advanced and competent. I am also a trance Medium which I hasten to add is not how many would imagine such practices to be! Many have a misconception of how a modern-day trance would be. I personally do not use trance in a public forum, I use it as a tool to teach others in a development capacity, that is my personal choice, but it is an amazing experience to watch a Medium truly in trance, to be so privileged to have visitors from the wonderful world of spirit come through to talk and pass on their knowledge with us is, for me, remarkable.

There is so much for us to learn from them and in my experience, they are always happy to come through to share their knowledge with us. I must also add that it is not an easy thing to learn to achieve, it takes a great deal of trust and patience to be able to get to that controlled state. It goes against all that the human mind and body can understand and accept, hence the great deal of trust needed, to allow another energy that of spirit to enter and take over control of your body is indeed naturally alien to us and there is always that initial fear of letting go of control of your own body. It can often take a long time to achieve but once achieved is wondrous. For my part I can only explain how it is for me, it is a very unusual sensation when someone else takes over all control of your body, your breathing, movement, literally everything to an extent that you can no longer move freely unless they choose you to!

This is something that should never be tried by anyone unless you are in a controlled environment with a more experienced teacher in my opinion, as on occasions things can go very wrong. But in the right environment it can be an amazing and rewarding experience, both for the Medium in trance and for the group watching. There are of course different states of trance. There are those who in effect may appear to have gone to sleep and may remember nothing when the session is over, there is also another state of trance where you are aware of what's being said, it's a bit like you are floating above your own body at times but you can also physically feel the presence of the teacher or Guide that has come to share their knowledge with you within the body.

A very strange experience I cannot deny but one that over time I have got used to and am happy to share for the rewards are truly worth it. Of course trance cannot be confused with Possession, that is a totally different thing, and is something that is not accepted willingly and can in cases happen to anyone in life. These cases are usually caused by an unpleasant entity and can be extremely frightening especially for those who may have to witness such a horrible thing but more so for the person that has been taken over involuntarily. I have had a few experiences of this in my lifetime and have been approached to help, usually in the early stages, but these are very different from 'attachments'.

I'm sure you have all seen many horror films that have been based on possession, indeed many are based on such incidences in life, no doubt a little embroidered for the sake of sensationalism and entertainment, but often are based on true stories. Well as I said previously, I have come across a few cases in my time and have been called upon to remove these nasty entities and thankfully once removed the person will return to normality. But what we need to remember is that often these entities are invoked by us! On occasions through using such things as Ouija Boards or 'home-made' versions, over time there have been many such 'games' introduced that work from the same basis, these props used are often done in a sense of fun and joking to see if they actually work! The sad thing is they often do but you need to remember when using such things you are connecting on a basic psychic level, calling out to any entity to join you and that is where the problem begins. There is no control over who or what can approach you and there are many darker entities that are all too willing to come and play your game with you. The problem there though is they rarely want to leave you and the ensuing problems can be terrifying. So my advice to anyone thinking of trying out these things is... Don't!

So I have covered a few ways that Mediumship can be used, but there are more of course but as I said before it takes many years of devoted work to the spirit world to achieve many of them safely. In a simpler way there is so much that can be achieved, I have found that the most wonderful gift that connection with the spirit world can give you is one of an overwhelming sense of love, which of course is the most important gift of all and indeed the most powerful.

In troubled times we need to remember to send our love not only to spirit but to the world itself and to heal the world. As I write this we are in the midst of the global pandemic, that of the Coronavirus Covid-19, very troubling and frightening times for us all, all over the world. I for one and as I know so many throughout the world are praying for help and healing for all of us, and at such times as these I have no doubt that many are praying and not just for themselves but for everyone. In times of stress, anxiety and fear it is what we all do, and it is indeed the most powerful thing of all.

Our hearts turn to love and compassion it is a very emotional time for all and a very sad one too for so many that have lost their lives and gone home to the spirit world, but there is great power in prayer and love for each other and that will see us through this terrible and trying time. It is sad that it takes such things to bring us together to such a level, but it is what will see us through it and bring us out the other side. For spirit hear us and will be there for us. I do hope that when we get through this we continue to remember this and I truly feel that there will be a change in this world.

I only pray that it will last, this feeling of love, unity and compassion for that is what will make significant change that this world needs at this time. Already we are seeing the earth healing itself restoring itself in all its beauty and glory, let's hope that we honour what is happening and take steps now to prevent the damage mankind has done to the planet and the animal kingdom. Such beauty in this world that is slowly dying from pollution, it is not just the flora and fauna that is suffering it is humankind too, so let us hope that we learn the lessons we need to learn from this terrible time and try to ensure that we make a difference for the future of all of us and our planet.

We all have a healing gift within us too, for we are spirit so draw the energy from within, whenever it is needed, and ask God and the realms of the spirit world to help. Feel the love and energy inside of you and send it out whether it be to an individual or to the earth itself, for we are all in need, your prayers will be answered but most of all you will feel the power of love yourself. Sometimes it is as if your heart will burst out of your chest and sometimes you will feel the happiness from within and the contentment it brings, but with all you will feel the gratitude of spirit and the love within which is truly a wonderful thing.

I often find that it is easier to visualise the healing you wish to send if you are sending healing remotely. Try to sit quietly for a few moments, imagine in your minds' eye the person you wish to help or if sending healing to the planet visualise that, then imagine it or the person surrounded in a beautiful blue healing light, then ask the spirit world to send their healing. Not only are you doing a worthwhile thing for others, but you will hopefully find a few moments of contentment yourself and a feeling of calm and peace which is all too rare in this bustling world we now live in.

Many people that do this, which yes, is a form of meditation, often say that they feel better for it and feel refreshed themselves too, for as you send out healing you too will receive it. So it is good for the body and the soul on all levels.

Chapter 12

In this world we live in now it is a changing world constantly with many up's and down's of course but such is life in general for us all. At this time I believe we need more stability, the world changes so quickly at times it is hard to keep up with it and at times it can seem everything is moving far too quickly. What we need is to take a step back sometimes to take stock of where we are, who we are and of course where we would like to be.

It isn't easy though is it? When things move and change so quickly we often get caught up in life and it's situations, barely giving us time to breath let alone think! The best thing we can do for ourselves and those around us is to stop, just every now and then and breathe. We need to allow ourselves that time even if it is brief to reset ourselves, to take stock and to think. It is the only way at times we are able to get some clarity in our lives.

I have found the best way to do this, for me, is to sit quietly, close your eyes and meditate even if it is only for a matter of minutes, take it slow and slow down your mind to enable you to think. In slowing our thought process it will also slow the body which is as important as slowing the mind. So relax, think of somewhere beautiful to be or just your 'happy place', even with five or ten minutes of this it will help to create calm. Allow yourself to feel the tensions slipping away, the muscles in your body relaxing. Surprisingly once you have managed to attain this you will feel calmer and refreshed.

This is also very useful if you feel yourself not only stressed but feel yourself getting angry with a situation or indeed a person in particular. I believe we all need to learn at times when to pull away and not allow our emotions to take over us in a bad way. Many a time I have felt frustrated with life or people and I have learnt now to pull back, and for me, I ask spirit to come close to me and heal me, to help alleviate those negative feeling from within. And let's face it we all have them! None of us are perfect and we do need to take control of ourselves and our emotions especially if they are negative.

Spirit have a wonderful way of helping us in every way when we ask for their help and guidance, but to do this we have to open to them to allow the healing energies and their overwhelming love to flood through. Those feelings are well worth allowing yourself to adapt to and to let them work in a positive manner, the benefits I assure you are totally worthwhile. Our loved ones, friends, Guides and Helpers are all there to help us when we request their help be it for ourselves or others they will do the very best they can, for they are love, positivity and kindness and they are more than happy to help and send these things to us in abundance. There is so much we can learn from spirit but we need to allow ourselves to listen and connect with them, I'm not saying that we all need to become working Mediums to do this, not at all, but if we allow ourselves to become more spiritual and listen to that inner voice within we will reap the benefits. For we are all of spirit and we are connected we just have to learn again how to connect even in a small way, it will change lives and change our way of thinking in many ways, but all for the greater good of us all.

I know that all this may sound simple but in fact it is, I am and always have been a great believer in the simplicity of all things spiritual and that is because spirit have taught me these things, taught me that whatever I do on my spiritual pathway it needs to be done in its simplicity. Whether I am teaching development and over many years of doing so I am always reminded by spirit to do so, in turn it makes it easier to learn and doesn't become complicated! It is often people and people's ideas that make it more complicated, for if you truly listen to spirit they will guide you truthfully, honestly and in simplicity.

As human beings we have a tendency to complicate things for ourselves, I don't know why but we do and we also have a tendency to overthink things, maybe it's the way we have evolved, to believe if something can be simply done it cannot be effective, in some cases this may be true but when it comes to spirit and our spirituality it doesn't need to be so. So many times I am reminded of this by my Guides and teachers and so far for me it has worked, I truly am happy to live a simpler life where I can! It is not spirit that complicates life, it is us.

I hope that as we grow now in this ever-changing world that we will come to a realisation of this and begin to change the way we think and behave, especially to each other, for we shall grow spiritually, it is already happening, it is who we are and what we are and that cannot change, it is more how we perceive ourselves and allow ourselves to change as we move forward in this world. It is indeed our free will that allows us to do bad things and think bad thoughts, as I have said before we all have two sides to us the good and the bad, and for many it is a constant struggle to maintain the goodness in us. However the majority do and that is why there is far more good in our world than evil.

Positivity is the key, inner strength is another, albeit at times and in the face of such dire circumstances going on in the world it is hard to stay positive and find that inner strength, but we all have it there we just need to dig a little deeper on these occasions to find it; and do not forget at these times in life to ask the spirit world for their help in allowing you to find it within and to find inner peace too. They will be more than happy to help you, you just have to trust in them and in yourselves.

There are so many people today and indeed always have been, searching for something, a way forward in life, a belief in something that some do not even know what or why, and I believe that our spirit within is trying to lead us to open ourselves to spirituality which as I have said before for me is not a religion but is a way of life. We all search for that peace and guidance where there is chaos and unrest, it is who we are to truly want that inner peace and a knowledge that we will go on after the body has expired, it cannot be for nothing and end when the body has had enough. I am often asked this question and of course it isn't the end of us at all it is another beginning.

We move on in a different form but with a higher consciousness a greater knowledge and awareness. It is a time for us to learn and understand this, to be more aware, it is the only way that this world will grow and move forward, to bring about a new world but one of positive love, kindness and compassion for each other and all things. spirit are coming ever closer to us, many more are becoming aware of this and many more are searching, looking for something, looking for fulfilment and searching for themselves.

It is time, time for us to become aware to grow

and to make changes. I'm not saying that we will become spiritual beings overnight of course not, that part is up to us, but as the spirit world come closer and join with us and share with us it will and is changing our perspectives and that is a positive thing. Any change that is required will take time, a long time to achieve for that is human nature. But all things are possible and I truly believe those changes are beginning and with each small step it is of great benefit to all humankind.

All things are possible for us and in time I truly believe we will take those steps forward into a new beginning on this earth, it may indeed take many more years to attain but I am optimistic that we are on the right pathway and it is a pathway that is destined for us all; to make a better world for us, to bring us closer to who we truly are and we can only do that with spirits help and a determination within to do so.

Chapter 13

To move forward and expand our consciousness will never and has never truly been easy for the human race, so many things to deal with in life and to cloud our judgement. This world we live in moves at a very fast pace, through things we have created, technology itself plays a large part in our lives. Social media has taken over too, a desire to constantly be posting everything we do and to see what everyone else is doing has taken over especially with the young, it has become addictive. Any addiction is not necessarily a healthy thing, especially when the moments we need to take for ourselves, our families and friends are compromised, leaving no time for the truly important things we need in our lives, and sometimes that is to just take stock and breathe.

We have convinced ourselves that in our spare moments we need to be checking on social media be it Facebook, Instagram, Twitter, Snapchat and so on, there are so many! But if we could only take a little more time for each other and for ourselves we would truly appreciate the things we already have in our lives and realise the true importance of that. Also that it is important to rest the mind as well as the body and the only way we can do that is by taking those moments to sit in the peace with your own thoughts, and by sharing time with those we love.

Who knows one day we will find the way to do this and have no need for social media, I'm not saying it is bad, in small doses it's ok, but how often do you stop and look around you and all we see is head's buried in phones. We miss so much that goes on around us too there is so much beauty out there, the planet we live on is indeed full of such beauty and wondrous things that we have so taken for granted in our ever-changing world, the pace it grows is often quite alarming and here we are rushing around getting caught up.

But everything we need is here in front of us. Yes

we have to work to live and yes we may enjoy it too, but always there is more, just listen to your heart and inner spirit and it will guide you to a place of peace and contentment too.

This is a place where we thrive, not just personally but as the human race, in all we need to find the balance and with everything that we are there is always a balance. Find the balance in your life and you will find peace and contentment that will bring you a greater sense of being and in turn your own true spirituality. I have found of late especially with the global pandemic the Coronavirus, that has made the world slow down, stop and think, spend time with our families, also to realise how much we love and miss those we cannot be with a that time. It has given us time to think, to rest, I'm not saying it is all good of course not we are having to deal with death in alarming numbers, losing those closest to us our family and friends, but I do believe that out of all these terrible times there will come some good.

If we cannot see that then what is it all for? We suffer truly, but our lives can become better, from the ashes rises the Phoenix and if we cannot see and make a change to our world then do we accept it was all in vain? It is not human nature to do that, we are strong and will, I truly hope, learn from this in a greater and more positive way.

Look at the earth itself healing itself so quickly without the pollution we pour into it and are indeed slowly destroying and poisoning our planet. Let us hope we have learned many lessons from this time and it will truly be a time that will never be forgotten, and a time we will always remember and be thankful to so many, those that worked tirelessly and in love to save so many lives even whilst risking their own. That is true humanity.

In adversity we rise and we shine again and when it is over we shall do so again, but let us not forget what has happened and fall back into our old ways, remember how we could take time to enjoy nature around us, hearing the birds sing even louder than before, seeing the skies bright and clear, smelling the purity of the air, seeing the waters clearer, the fish returning to places they had long ago abandoned. Spending time with the children and our families appreciating them more, all these things are important and always will be. All these things bring us closer to spirituality and there is where we find our peace.

Love and laughter are the things that also bring us happiness and are very important for our well-being, sharing our lives, our thoughts, our passions are indeed important to us too and we need to embark on all these things in life to fulfil us, for they bring about that feeling of well-being within us, so let us hope that we always remember to partake in all these things and to try to remove the negativity in our lives.

Sadly there are many who are negative, of course we all have our moments, none of us are perfect or can be in that permanent state of mind, such is life itself on occasions, but I truly feel sorry for those in this world who have and live a negative life. As I mentioned before we all have a darker side and a lighter side to us, but if you allow the darkness to overcome then we live in a very different place. For some it is a medical condition and may need help for that, but for some it is a negative train of thought that brings them to wish to harm others or take away their happiness or indeed to destroy what others have achieved or indeed have.

I have come across many people that live with this train of thought unfortunately, some you can help and some you cannot, and I understand that in these cases sometimes you will have to walk away from them to stop you from experiencing the pain that they inflict. I truly feel sorry for such people and all we can do to help is to continue to ask spirit for healing for them, for they truly need healing and help.

It is sad that they do not realise not just the pain they inflict upon others, but the pain they inflict upon themselves. I have encountered many like this sadly and I have often found that with this constant negativity they draw nothing but negativity to them. If you send out love to all then you will surely receive love back in abundance for it is the positivity of it. If you send out negativity and wish harm to others, then I'm afraid ultimately that is all you shall receive back over time.

It is also the worst thing you can do in life, for all you will attract from the spirit world is the dark entities that are waiting for people like this, to latch on to and create even more darkness in this world. Also it is possible to send such dark thoughts to another person and with that a dark entity will attach itself to the person in question, which in turn creates a great deal of problems for them, in many cases they will need clearing.

As I mentioned earlier an 'attachment' can inflict itself upon someone through no fault of their own it can happen randomly but also through another's dark thoughts. However it is a foolish pathway to walk, to send evil to another, for in my experience I have found that those who strive to do such things, will only find themselves in a similar position. What you send out you shall receive back ultimately, for we all have lessons to learn and some will learn the harder way.

I have been asked many times by people that have experienced such attachments if they have been cursed. It seems more and more these thoughts are more pronounced in this day and age, strange in many ways as I would like to think we have progressed further in this world, but in many cultures throughout the world such practices are indeed still around. I often hear also of people especially younger people being drawn into Satanic practices and cults, that concerns me a great deal.

I have on occasions been asked to clear someone

that has managed to free themselves of such groups but found themselves with a dark and demonic presence with them, it seems they do not like to lose such members of their cults. I will never understand why anyone would wish to engage in such practices but one thing I am very sure of, that is the power of good will always overpower the practices of evil.

Curses are often effective only by the fear they invoke in people, the power of the mind is a very powerful thing and can create a very detrimental environment for anyone that has been affected by such practices. The more we allow these thought into our minds the more problems they will cause, but in some cases the practices used will summon demonic and evil entities to plague another.

These entities can be removed and destroyed but sometimes the hardest part is convincing the mind that the person is free of them. That can often take time to heal, but thankfully in most cases it is an instant feeling of relief and acceptance and often an instant knowing that they are free of the entity, for the presence of such a being is often an intense negative feeling and knowing.

Thankfully there are more that will never experience this kind of encounter than those that will, for there truly is more positivity than negativity in this world. So think twice when you are having those feelings, when you are angry with someone, do not wish them harm for you never know what you might attract not only to them but to yourself, for what you send you may receive and that truly is not worth the negative energy that you create. Think of forgiveness, think of positive thoughts, for your well-being as well as theirs.

Chapter 14

One of the most often talked about subjects with regard to spiritual matters is the animal kingdom, so often the question arises, "*Are animals spiritually connected?*". Well, yes, very much so. Our animals see hear and sense spirit around but are also living creatures that also have a spirit, so are therefore very aware of spirit in all forms. It's a little like children that see all and hear all things are so accepting of spirit through their innocence and natural abilities at such early ages; well animals are very much the same, not through their age of course but because of their natural ability and their trusting and accepting nature, they have no-one to convince them otherwise!

It is very interesting to watch, as I mentioned earlier, when a spirit will enter your home, as they frequently do and your pet will suddenly be aware of their energy, usually their ears will prick up and sometimes they may whine or grumble and look at something you cannot see, often with dogs they will wag their tails and bark as they will indeed hear spirit talking to them and this is always a positive sign, they will usually settle very quickly in these cases and be comfortable with the presence there.

Sometimes they may also be aware of a past pet that is now in spirit, for they too often come to revisit us, again you may not see them but any pet in your household surely will. There may be an initial few moment of distrust but again usually your pet will settle quickly and accept the intrusion of another readily. One of the interesting things about animals is that they will also detect the presence of something that is not good and their reaction will be of a very different nature. If a darker more unpleasant spirit enters, your pet will react in a very different way, either by growling or hissing and moving into a more aggressive mode to protect its domain and to warn you of such an intruder.

However if the entity is a more powerful one you may see your pet display fear and run and hide, which is a normal reaction too; I mean wouldn't you? Animals are a good guide and insight into who is visiting your home and are extremely spiritually aware. It is also possible to connect with animals especially for a Medium or indeed anyone who has empathy for them and indeed for each other. I have often been asked to give healing to animals which of course am happy to do so and on many occasions picked up what ails them.

This is indeed handy to determine why a pet is under the weather but it is possible also to communicate with them through spirit Guides and also family in spirit who are far more equipped to connect with animals than we are. It takes time and development of course for us to learn how to connect, indeed as it does for us to learn to connect with our loved ones in the spirit world, but all things are possible with perseverance, trust and a desire to do so.

I have heard many stories of 'unusual' behaviour from pets especially dogs that have apparently for no reason sat up, tail wagging, and performing a few tricks, when no command has been given by its owner. But the command has indeed been given by someone in spirit, the connection is there and the dog can hear every command and is happy to perform for its visitor. Such is the beauty of the connection between animals and the spirit world.

An animal senses and indeed uses its senses far more than we do, it lives by its senses, so it is a natural thing for them. Also they can sense your energy they know instinctively if you mean them harm, if you are afraid of them and react accordingly, but they also know if you are kind, they can sense a loving caring nature in people, hence why a pet will react positively or aggressively to a stranger. They are very good judges of character that I have certainly grown to accept and acknowledge, and have frequently seen and had my own suspicions confirmed!

Your pet can be the friendliest good-natured pet ever, but if they come across someone that is, shall we say a little dubious or maybe not what they appear to be to you, your pet will certainly let you know and make a hasty retreat or indeed growl when it is not usually in their nature to do so. So take heed of your animals they can tell you more than you realise! They are our allies and only wish to protect you and themselves of course. Apart from giving you their unconditional love, they are a joy to us in more ways than we often realise.

Of course not all animals are naturally friendly, wild animals of course have no connection or interaction with us so naturally we are seen as a threat to them, even so they will still sense your energy around you, the energy that your aura projects from you; but our domestic animals although used to the presence of us humans, will still be guided by their sense of smell and by the energy you have.

For domestic dogs, especially those that are

devoid of regular human contact or treated badly, may become aggressive, which is against their natural behaviour, but it is what they have been trained to do. Especially a dog that has been cruelly bred for fighting or some guard dogs are taught to behave in this way, sadly they are trained to override the natural ability to connect with us on a more spiritual energy - a little like human beings too that do not wish to connect with their own spirituality. It doesn't mean that they cannot still see spirit, if spirit choose them to, but if the mind is conditioned in such a way the connection sadly is often lost. But there is always hope with time, love and perseverance all living things can learn to reconnect with their own spirituality.

To go a little deeper into our energy field around us, this is our aura, we all have an aura and all living things have an aura too. Our aura is the energy that comes from inside us, from our spirit within, the stronger the spirituality we have the stronger the aura glows and we can project this energy to use it to touch others, to protect ourselves from darker energies too. It is mostly common that our aura shows itself as a purer white or golden light around us, for those that have learnt to see them, and you can learn to see them, and also some have learnt to read auras too.

I'm sure many of you have often noticed a kind of glow around someone's head? That is the aura, in some an aura can glow very brightly and seem very pronounced around them this usually means that this person is somewhat more connected spiritually, but we all have one! Often these can also be seen in different colours, which is how many have learnt to 'read' it. Once you have learnt what the colours mean it becomes easier to find out more about a person, the colours are usually coinciding with the colours of the Chakras which will explain the energy they are projecting at that time.

Have you ever met someone for the first time

and for no reason you can explain have an instant feeling about them? In some it can be an instant attraction or feeling of being comfortable in their presence, even without speaking to them first? Or on the other hand you have taken an instant dislike to someone again without knowing why? We often put this down to our 'gut instinct' but it is also that your auras have connected and it has sent the message back to you to either accept them or be wary of them and it never fails you if you listen to that inner feeling you get.

A person, shall we say, that is not of a good nature or indeed a good person can exude a darker aura, this can often be seen as grey in colour or sometimes even darker, dependent on the person in question. This darker energy will instinctively tell you that they are not good to be around that is why you get that feeling that you just want to walk away or indeed get as far away as possible! If this is not possible then be wary and listen to those feelings you have for they are for good reason. The sense of ease that you feel with others also are usually true too, for it is what lies within a person that exudes out from them into the aura, and those with a good heart and good intentions will always instinctively make you feel comfortable in their presence.

It is also possible to learn to project your aura as you learn to develop your spirituality and as you become stronger the spirit within grows and therefore also becomes stronger. Your aura will then not only grow brighter but will expand and become wider. For those that develop mediumistic abilities or indeed that practice and walk any kind of spiritual pathway will find that the aura grows with you as you progress. Children have a natural beautiful energy that shines bright as for in their childhood they are usually pure of heart and certainly pure of spirit.

It is only as we get older that life can take over us and also other people's opinions and fears that cause us to think and act differently that we can lose a little of the natural spirituality that we are born with. I truly believe that no child is born evil, evil is created by us and this world we live in.

We all have two sides to us one that is darker and one that is light, thankfully most of us will allow the light to shine and we fight the darker side of us, we can never allow that to win for it goes against all that we are and have been created for. We are human and have human thoughts and none of us are perfect by any means but we are judged not by the thoughts we have but by the deeds we do. So remember to fight the darkness and continue into the light, we can create positivity and a better world if we do, and your aura will shine brighter than you could ever imagine and touch all those around you with your light.

I would also like to add that although some may listen to the darker side of their nature and indeed act upon it, to go against all that we are is a sad pathway to embark on and will leave you more inclined to attract the darker entities that surround our world which will hinder any return to a path of light and love, but there is redemption there, we can turn ourselves around to that path but only if we truly mean to and wish to. Actions of course will speak far louder than words.

The spirit within you is one of light and always will be, it is the spirit we came into this world with and the one we shall leave it with too. It is only the human mind and body that allows us to change and for some, do awful deeds but spirit will always help us to change but to do so we have to want to do so for as always we have free will. We cannot undo the bad or evil things that are done but there is always atonement, we can never change our past but we can change our future for the time we have left on this planet. So it is never too late to try again. Only we can atone for our own deeds, it is not enough to just ask for forgiveness but we have to show that we deserve it and have earned it in the eyes of our God and of humanity. For only when we return home to the spirit world is forgiveness truly given once earned.

Once you return home to spirit there will be an Awakening, a re-joining of consciousness of all that you are and have been through many lives, a realisation of why you were here in this life and the lessons you have learned, for some there may be a healing time of adjustment especially if this life had not gone in the way it was meant to have been; if we had chosen to walk a very different pathway and carried out deeds that were against all that we are and meant to be, a path that has gone against all that spirituality, kindness and love is, the spirit will need a time of healing and rest and in some cases realisation.

We all return to the same place to the spirit world, not heaven or hell in the basic of terms, but we return from where we came, however there are as I mentioned before different levels within that world that we are striving to attain. The better a person we were and learned what we needed to learn in this life and indeed every life, the more and higher we progress there. So think twice before you act, or how you treat someone in life for all that you do ultimately reflects on you and only you are accountable for your actions.

For it is also inevitable that should we not learn the lessons we came to this earth to learn or fulfil our purpose here, then at some point we will return into another life, it could be a very different kind of life but it will be one that will enable us to learn again those lessons even if in a different format. The ultimate goal is for us to evolve and progress spiritually and also to enable the human race and earth to progress too.

With the changes occurring now I do believe more and more people are gaining a greater understanding of these things, even subconsciously in some cases but a greater knowing and indeed a thirst for knowledge and understanding too - it is what stirs inside us. So continue to listen to that little voice in your head and heart, the good one of course, it will lead you to your true path and destiny and the rewards will be greater ultimately.

Chapter 15

So hopefully so far I have given you some insight into the wonderful world of spirit, but most of all I hope that some of the fear that follows this pathway has been taken away, for truly there is nothing to fear from a spiritual path and indeed I feel it is more important for us to open our eyes to all possibilities and realisations that we are spirit ourselves, and in the normal way of life there is nothing to fear and certainly death is not an ending to our life, but a new beginning and a new Awakening to another life.

One that we came from and inevitably will return to, but a life of love, beauty, peace and enlightenment and one certainly not to be feared but ultimately revered. None of us wish to leave this earth necessarily but it has always been a human fear that we move on to nothing, that death is an ending with nothing more and our greatest fears are that we leave our families and loved ones behind.

Of course we must physically leave them but we will always be connected spiritually, we can return whenever we choose to visit our families, to watch over them and keep an eye on them, to watch them progress in their lives and finally be there to meet them when they too return home to the spirit world to be reunited with us.

I truly believe that as we open our understanding to spirit and our own spirituality we progress as human beings, and as we progress we learn to open our minds and hearts to it and we will all in time be able to communicate with our loved ones that are in the spirit world.

For we must now move forward, our salvation lies in a spiritual pathway, which is why the Awakening has begun and will continue to progress through the coming years and the next generations.

However we must begin now, the world must change and I believe that it surely will with the help and guidance of spirit not just our families and loved ones but from those from the higher realms that are coming ever closer to us, to educate us and to open us to their world and to a realisation of who we are and indeed where we came from. So many already are waking up to this reality and acceptance but we have a long way to go.

In truth there will always be a negative presence be it human or spiritual for we feed them with our negative deeds and thoughts and until we can try to eradicate those, which is not easy as we are after all human, but in time? Who knows, I believe we can. We are not perfect and neither are we expected to be but when we listen to that inner voice that says something is wrong that is when we make a change to this world, we fight the inner demons and allow the light to shine through for there is more light than dark within us and we must allow the light to win.

So for now when you feel drawn to spirituality and have questions do not be afraid to ask and do not be afraid to allow yourselves to open your own connection to spirit, it will not happen overnight and many of us need to be guided on this path, as I have said before you do not have to develop these abilities to become a Medium as such but enough to open and accept that spirit exists and to respect them and yourselves.

Many are being drawn now to spirituality because your own spirit, your soul, is waking and growing stronger so listen to it and ask spirit for guidance in life; I don't mean with questions such as will I marry or will I have money, but ask for help, for guidance and healing for yourselves and for each other, for the earth itself, for all those that suffer and for those less fortunate than yourself for the power to do so is out there we just need to trust and accept that it is.

Should you decide to develop your abilities, or enhance your knowledge, and we all can, then find someone to teach you and guide you on that pathway, it is not easy to do so alone and there are many good teachers out there that have the knowledge and have dedicated their lives to spirit and their teachings. But know that the true teachings of spirit are those that are simplicity itself, there is no need for complex or complicated ways, a simple path is one of truth and one that spirit are always willing for us to follow.

Start at the beginning, do not try to rise to grander or higher levels before you have begun for you will miss so much and always listen to your inner self, which will help to guide you, if something doesn't feel right or sit right then it isn't right, not for you. There is so much trust needed too not only for you to trust in spirit but to trust in your teacher and do not try to run before you can walk. It is a long process but well worth the time and effort you put in to develop such gifts.

One day I do believe that we will all rise to higher spiritual levels, we will all use the gifts that we were born with but have forgotten, there will be no more fear of such things and it will be the new normal, we will be able to communicate in such ways that we never dreamt of and I also believe that we will be able to do so with each other not just with spirit. When we communicate with spirit it is a form of telepathy, communication comes through the mind for as a Medium communication is by seeing, hearing or feeling and those processes are through the mind itself, so if we can do that and accept this then what is to say that we cannot develop these abilities further to use with each other? Often people are so connected and when connected especially by love it deepens that connection.

How often do you seem to know what your partner or child is thinking? To finish another's sentence? It is from the connection you have, a deep spiritual one, so imagine taking that further and being able to do so to a greater capacity! The human brain we know uses such a small percentage of its capacity and maybe one day we will learn to develop it to a greater potential.

It is often believed that a Medium uses a part of the brain that we have learnt to access to enable communication with those in spirit, hence why many scientists are eager to do trials and tests on Mediums, people have been able in some cases to move objects with the mind, spirit can, so why can't we? I am indeed aware that we have a long way to go to achieve such goals, but if we open our minds to the possibilities?

There are of course some people that have achieved such amazing capabilities, the power of the mind is quite exceptional, we can learn to control pain and override it, there are so many possibilities for us, but for now we need to take one step at a time. The ability to connect with spirit though is an easier one but requires a re-awakening of the mind for we are born with this ability but through life and others' fears it is often shut down but can be opened again whenever we choose to do so.

Remember that all that is needed in this world is love, for love is stronger than any other emotion or feeling, it can be all consuming and all engulfing if we allow it to and there is no greater feeling than that. The spirit world lives only in love and truth and a kindness to all living beings and that is where we need to be to enable this world to heal and move forward.

It is the emotion that will change the world to make it better for all of us for what we send out to others we will in time receive it back, so focus on sending positive thought out to all, even those who have caused you harm for should you harbour negativity and hatred that is what will surround you in your life; it is destructive and will in turn attract the negative and destructive entities that are also out there, waiting for us to fail and to feed on it and drag us on their pathway. It is human for us to not forget when harm and pain has been inflicted on us but it is also a greater human capacity we have to forgive, and this is a positive force.

Forgiveness is not only good for our own well-being as believe me it will make you feel better than any harbouring of hatred, but we do have a greater ability to love in us it is first and foremost and the emotion that brings us contentment, happiness and peace within. It will also attract love and good things to you and wrap you up in its beauty.

Life is never easy but we can always make it better for ourselves, look to the future think positive thoughts for yourself and when bad things happen, learn from them don't let them hold you back, move forward and use the lessons you have learnt and also use them to help others on your pathway. This is our progression here on this earth, do not allow the bad to swallow you up and hold you back, stay positive always.

Listen to your inner spirit and let it guide you to a better place, a better life. Remember we are accountable for our own actions, only us, and only we can make amends for the wrongs we do, remember also that how we live our lives here will reflect on our spiritual progression when we go home to the spirit world, no we are not and not expected to be perfect, but we are expected to do our very best and be the best human being we can be.

With thoughts of love we can change the world, we can affect others and with collective love and positivity the world will become better, send out healing to the world, ask for change, ask for help, and spirit will be listening and willing to do so. spirit watch over us as we are their 'children', they wish only the very best for us and willingly help when we ask, but we must ask not expect, for we have free will and that will never change and spirit will always respect that too.

Live in the light always for it is who we were created to be. We may have lost our way somewhat at times but it is a pathway that is easy to find again.

I hope that you have gained some insight and a little more knowledge of all things spiritual and in turn this may have removed some of the fears that have been held for and about the wonderful world that is spirit.

Printed in Great Britain
by Amazon